Your Options

Proactive Thinking in an Uncertain World

Your Options

Proactive Thinking in an Uncertain World

"By failing to prepare, you are preparing to fail."

Ben Franklin

Luis A. Ramirez

Your Options: Proactive Thinking in an Uncertain World/Luis A. Ramirez.-First edition

1. Leadership. 2. Health & Safety. 3. Emergency & Disaster Management Policies. 4. Self-Help. 5. Risk Management

Independently published in the United States in 2019
On Amazon Kindle Direct Publishing

ISBN-13: 978-1688752665 (Paperback)
ISBN-10: 1688752668 (Paperback)
ASIN: 1688752668 (Paperback)
ASIN: B07X51SXQS (eBook)
Edited by Michael Palladino
Cover Designed by Ivanna F. Ciborowski

For the victims, families, and communities affected by gun violence.

For the brave law enforcement personnel who courageously and tirelessly continue to keep our communities safe.

And to the leaders who believe in the fundamental need and right to proactively train before an emergency strikes.

Contents

- This Page Left Blank Intentionally -

Foreword

Several years ago, I taught Luis A. Ramirez in a Master of Business program for senior executives. As he sat there in the back row, he immediately struck me as a charismatic executive with many diverse experiences that he could bring to the conversation—not only in terms of business and technical skills, but also as a veteran of the Marines, a highly disciplined ultramarathoner, and a new father.

In one exercise that focused on group creativity, I asked the students to design the classroom of the future, all within the high-pressure timeframe of fifteen minutes. Luis' exercise was one I will never forget: he had designed a classroom that he felt would safely protect our students from active shooters, as well as any other potential threats. It was far different from any of the other pictures produced by other groups–which included talented senior leaders in architecture, engineering, and medicine—and it is a picture I remember vividly to this day. For me, it was one of those wonderful moments in which the student becomes the teacher. I had set up what I thought was a 'fun' exercise; Luis saw the question in a far deeper way, grasping truly serious threats and picturing a way to defend against them. I have, in the years since, read articles on how schools are investing millions to equip their classrooms with protections just as Luis had envisioned.

It was a few years later that I realized that this insightful picture was not something Luis had created from thin air, but rather from decades of experience in military security. Luis informed me that he was starting his own company—Fidelis—to consult with businesses so that they may prepare for active shooter attacks and other unthinkable scenarios. I have been excited to see his business develop, and this book perfectly represents the intellectual capital behind it.

What you're about to read is a gift to any leader who wants to develop the foresight to think about these threats. While it is always easier to simply continue business-as-usual, we have no choice but to confront new realities today. I am glad that Luis will be that knowledgeable and accessible guide, so that he may help you navigate these most difficult scenarios and lead you to protect your business and your people.

Tanya Menon, PhD
- Professor of Management and Human Resources at Fisher College of Business, Ohio State University
- Author of *Stop Spending, Start Managing: Strategies to Transform Wasteful Habits*

Preface

Before we start, let's address the elephant in the room.

We're living in a time in which feelings of fear, numbness, and uncertainty can seem like an inescapable norm. Active shooter incidents have continuously terrorized many communities in the United States of America and left us all wondering whether we can ever truly feel safe again.

But the heaviness of not knowing if it will ever stop or slow down may be giving way to a more significant issue. The fear we feel may lead us down the path of further paralysis. But we must never forget the words that President Franklin Roosevelt gave us when the country was going through another crisis:

"We have nothing to fear but fear itself."

I strongly believe in gun safety. It is a responsibility I learned when I joined the United States Marine Corps at the age of eighteen. Part of the safety rules that were conveyed and expected to be memorized clearly stated that every weapon is to be treated as if it were loaded. We were also told that you never point a firearm at anything you do not intend to shoot. Pretty simple safety rules if you ask me.

This training became the catalyst for my crusade in providing security for everyone, and in time I began to see how the USMC safety protocols could be applied in a broader sense that could benefit us all.

In 2018 I started my risk mitigation company. I now hold seminars and private safety and security training sessions, with the goal of providing the public with the fundamental building blocks for situational awareness and safety preparedness. The main focus of the training has always been to provide strategic options one can implement during or prior to an active shooter situation in order to manage uncertainty, and I'd like to think that I've made a positive difference.

This experience with professional development training led me to the opportunity to publish this very book. I hope the content within these pages can assist people like yourself.

Stay aware. Stay vigilant. Stay safe.

Acknowledgments

I want to thank my wife and two children for their unwavering support while writing this book. Their commitment to understanding my passion for empowering at least one person in one location with this book was extraordinary. They showed grit and perseverance while supporting my vision to help against gun violence in whichever way I can.

My deepest gratitude for the unconditional, tireless, and exceptional editorial support goes to Michael Palladino. This book could not have been completed without his copyediting and proofreading. And I must give credit and thanks to the best ultramarathon pacer, Mishka Shubaly for connecting me to Michael. You helped me finish Vermont 100 and now this book.

Last but not least, to my friends, colleagues, and exceptional leaders who have supported my request to read the first draft of the manuscript – thank you. You had more important things to do, yet you were willing to support me through the process. To Tanya Menon, for her willingness and availability to writing the foreword to the book. She has inspired me to continue developing as a leader. And to the remarkable people I have met during the professional development training sessions I have held throughout the country. This book grew out of those experiences and your candid feedback.

- This Page Left Blank Intentionally -

Part One

Your Journey to a Proactive State of Mind

"Intuition is like reading a word without having to spell it out."

Agatha Christie, Murder at the Vicarage

1

The Essential Elements

"In any moment of decision, the best thing you can do is the right thing. The worst thing you can do is nothing."

Theodore Roosevelt

Proactiveness

All horrific incidents, whether deliberately caused or purely accidental, have a distinct advantage. The element of surprise is always on their side.

If you're in a public area, living your life and minding your own business, a life-or-death situation is likely to be one of the furthest things from your mind. But we have all seen the news lately, and we are well aware that certain incidents seem to be on the rise, specifically mass shootings within the United States of America.

When you see these stories in the media, you're likely to ask yourself what you would do to survive such an event. You might mentally put yourself in that type of a crisis and try to imagine how you'd help victims while also helping yourself. You can speculate and strategize all you like, but if you actually did find yourself in one of these situations, would you be ready? Furthermore, if you're in a position of oversight and leadership, what steps could you take to prevent the danger from striking your business and staff?

These incidents, by their very nature, are meant to catch you off-guard and terrorize innocent people. And the unfortunate truth is, they almost always succeed in doing so. There is no such thing as complete preparation. The element of surprise is just too powerful and advantageous for any act of terror. Fortunately, it does have a formidable nemesis, one that serves as your greatest ally: a proactive state of mind.

Developing, maintaining, and engaging society with a proactive state of mind is the most crucial set of tools you could possibly have, no matter if it's in the context of instilling preventative measures or as a matter of immediate survival.

Merriam-Webster defines the word "proactive" as:

- *relating to, caused by, or being interference between previous learning and the recall or performance of later learning.*
- *acting in anticipation of future problems, needs, or changes.*

The goal of this book is to engrain proactive behaviors into your instincts and awareness. By doing so, you will develop and maintain your skills to anticipate and observe changes within your environment. Think of it as amplifying and augmenting your mental model. Mental models are frameworks you've developed over time to help you interpret how the world works and understand the relationships between things. By developing a proactive state of mind, your mental model will become reinforced with the unique experiences that you have attained in life, which will assist you in connecting the dots. I encourage you to utilize these prior experiences and combine them with the information presented in this book. By doing so, you can continue to build on your mental model, which will help develop a game plan in anticipation of danger.

But constructing this mental model isn't where the process ends. It must be maintained. Think of it as a shield. To someone who is unskilled and unfamiliar with such a thing, the shield might as well be just one large and cumbersome hunk of metal. However, someone who has taken the time to learn not only how to use it effectively and keep it at its prime condition now has the power to create their destiny.

Throughout this book, I will provide you with the knowledge you'll need to learn to use that metaphorical shield properly. You'll learn how to think at least one step ahead at all times. You'll learn why it's important to remain vigilant. You'll learn how to identify the warning signs. You'll learn the options that are available to you if danger strikes. Essentially, you'll learn how to properly maintain your "shield" so it will be primed and ready.

Intuition

Intuition is powerful. It may not be visible or tangible, but we all can sense whether something is within the norm or outside it. It's the gut feeling we get when something is not right. People always rely on their intuition when making choices throughout the course of their day. Many people are in tune with their own intuition, but some others are too preoccupied to pay attention to any potential risks.

Everyone is born with the foresight that is required to detect forms of danger, even without having a full comprehension of their particular magnitude. It's not unlike a radar system, in that it helps us detect environmental or human-caused threats that surround us. If our alarm goes off, we must decide whether the threat means we must either evade, create a barricade, defend, attack, notify authorities, or even take it upon ourselves to investigate and determine if it's simply a false alarm.

Consider children's strengths or weaknesses within their sense of intuition. If they notice something that is abnormal to them, their intuition kicks into gear almost immediately. A child's intuitive strength allows them to amplify their curious minds, thus enhancing their respective mental model. In fact, this strength can be so powerful that it almost negates any weaknesses the child has with their intuition. Since their minds are perpetually curious and wide open to new information, they can easily learn from any past mistakes they may have made in identifying possible dangers.

For example, my two-year-old son is always exploring the world and absorbing information through every experience, no matter how minor it may seem to you or I. He's often very focused on the matter at hand, taking in any detail that comes in front of him, which is then stored as a piece of data in his mental database.

One of the cartoons he particularly enjoys is called *BabyBus*. The show focuses on meeting the educational needs of preschool children while embracing safety as its core mission. One day, our fire alarm went off while I was cooking. My son stopped what he was doing and reacted by instructing us "not to panic," and to prepare to evacuate. I was amazed at the level of data he absorbed by watching the show titled Baby Panda's Fire Evacuation on *BabyBus* (BabyBus, 2018). He recognized danger by relying on the mental model he learned from the show, even though he didn't have any "real world" perspective. His intuition kicked in, and he reacted accordingly.

All adults have the same intuitive capability that children possess, but at some point, complacency kicks in, and this ability becomes minimized. As we get older, our sense of intuition may begin to dull. Adults have built a habit of trying to analyze sudden danger before considering whether to take any action.

Take the August 3, 2019, El Paso shooting, for example. According to witnesses, a child ran inside a nearby store and told shoppers, "there's an active shooter at Walmart." Initially, no adult took the child's notification seriously enough. Sadly, the child's message was spot-on, but the adult's intuition had to be validated before taking any action. But by then, it was too late. (O'Kane, 2019)

Please understand that it is risky to dismiss any threat indicators or variables. We should attempt to remove any predetermined bias, such as:

"There is no danger where I am."

"This is a safe town."

"That only happens in big cities, not in my rural hometown."

"I never thought something like this would happen here."

"It will never happen here/to me."

"I guess I never thought it could possibly happen here."

"We never thought it would be so close to us this time."

"You see on the news all the time, but you don't think it could happen here until it does."

"We never thought it would be so close to us this time."

"I didn't think something like this would ever happen to me, and especially not here."

Thinking like this can lay the foundation for a world of potential risks. If we aren't in tune with the variables that make up our surroundings, what good is intuition?

Never underestimate that funny feeling you get when you sense something is outside the norm. There's always a reason as to why your mental alarms should go off, whether you can put your finger on it or not. Trust that intuitive radar. Something like a child running into your immediate setting and notifying you of an active shooter should be taken very seriously. Verify if you must, but react immediately and accordingly.

Throughout the course of your life, there have been instances that shaped your sense of intuition on some level. It could have been something profoundly traumatic, or even something much more benign. It could have also been something positive, like the feeling you experienced when you finally mastered a skill you had been relentlessly practicing. Whatever it was, your subconscious made a note of it. You absorbed the data, analyzed it, and saved it to your mental hard drive because deep down you knew that it could prove valuable later. Without question, we are at a moment in history in which we should always be on high alert and listen to the mental data we've been able to accumulate.

Your intuition can't allow it to atrophy. It becomes less effective when we allow ourselves to become preoccupied or distracted. We seldom realize that our surroundings are largely made up of constantly changing forces of nature, people, or systems, each one of them acting as perpetual variables. Your point of view and ability to listen to your environment are strategic tools you can use to your advantage. Your ability to pick up on changes in your environment, be they obvious or subtle, is paramount. Doing so will help you use sights and sounds to improve your awareness and make split-second decisions during times of stress and uncertainty.

The Easter Sunday bombings that took place in Sri Lanka on April 21, 2019, serve as a prime example of this. These bombings were part of a coordinated attack which targeted Christians and tourists, resulting in over 300 deaths and over 500 injuries. (Khushbu Shah, 2019) If you have a look at the YouTube videos that show the moments before the bombing, you will notice how the variables within the environment are different. The individuals that executed these attacks were carrying what appeared to be extremely heavy backpacks. (GlobalNews, 2019) This may not be something to question since tourists typically wear backpacks in cities such as Sri Lanka, but the determination in their walk, in conjunction with the oversized bags, is a good indication that something is out of the norm.

In Chapter 3, you'll see examples of threat indicators you must pay attention to within your environment. Here is a preliminary list for you to consider throughout your day:

Mental Safety Checklist to Consider Throughout Your Day

1. Has the flow of people increased or decreased?
2. Compare how people are dressed. Is there anyone that stands out?
3. Observe the pace of the walk. Does anybody stand out?
4. Are the sounds you're listening to typical in relation to your setting?
5. Have things changed in the environment or the physical security of the property, such as doors being unlocked, left ajar, or pried open?
6. Do you know your exit route or exit doors?
7. Do you spot abnormal behavior?
8. Is anyone following you?

Complacency and Vigilance

When you get too comfortable, you get too complacent. And in the moments leading up to a potential life-or-death emergency, complacency kills. It leaves the door wide open for mishaps and missed opportunities in which to identify possible risks or threats. By settling into your comfort zone, you relinquish the ability to react to a situation, and you end up weakening your decision-making skills.

Perpetrators are always looking to exploit weaknesses and vulnerabilities. Once you show these signs, it may be too late. Always try not to let your guard down. Remain sharp and continuously aware of your surroundings. In a way, the comfort zone is in the same zip code as the danger zone.

The flip side of complacency is vigilance. It's important to recognize that vigilance doesn't mean paranoia. It's just the concept of remaining alert throughout the course of your day. You must scrutinize your surroundings by going down your mental checklist and use your intuition to ensure you remain at least one step ahead of any potential dangers.

Here are six examples of physical security features you may come across in public or private settings. By remaining vigilant and recognizing these physical security features within your surrounding environment, you can cut down on the risk factors and raise the odds of safety and survival.

Six Examples of Physical Security Features

1. Barriers

2. Physical security resources

3. Technology

4. Access control

5. Escort

6. Safety protocols

Barriers

Think of barriers as layers. These layers will bring an element of territoriality between you and others. Barriers can be considered natural or manmade. Natural barriers could be mountains, ditches, water, or any other obstacles that are geographical and difficult to cross. Manmade barriers are protective structures such as fences, walls, floors, roadblocks, signs, or other elements that impede a person's capability to reach you. Ideally, it should be difficult for anyone to penetrate a layer of security.

So if you're inside a building, you'll obviously be surrounded by walls, roofs, windows, doors, etc. These present opportunities for obstructing the path between yourself and the threat of danger, but the opposite can also be true. If you see a breach in the security feature, no matter what it may be, you must question it.

A prime example would be open doors in a particular area, one in which doors must be locked and secured, or if there is an object that is visually blocking an entryway. If the door is open, close it. If the door is physically blocked, try to remove that obstacle. This example is applicable in such environments as a school setting, a place of worship, or a movie theater. These are examples of vulnerabilities that weaken the physical security of any facility and can lead to you and those around you becoming potential targets.

Physical Security Resources

Physical security tends to be overlooked these days, or at least not taken as seriously as it once was. This is likely because more focus is placed on cybersecurity, or perhaps because of "budgetary" reasons. If there are no obstacles to impede potential perpetrators, you are making your organization, customers, assets, and personnel an easy target. To optimize and reinforce your facility's security, consider installing and utilizing fences, locks, access control cards, biometric access control systems, or fire suppression systems. Tactics like this will ensure that your facility and its inhabitants will be what's called a "hard target."

The term is self-explanatory. An active shooter has two advantages right off the bat. They have the element of surprise on their side and a deadly weapon in their hands. You must not overlook any possible measures or opportunities that will help make things more difficult for the perpetrator to carry out their plan.

Furthermore, your physical security features should be comprehensive and fully monitored. Seriously consider installing surveillance cameras and notification systems with intrusion detection sensors and/or heat sensors, if you haven't already. Strict policies and procedures should also be developed and tested with your personnel. These resources should not collect dust or die on the vine. The safety of your organization is far more important than the company budget.

Perpetrators are often very observant of how your physical security is conducted. They often test their plans by doing a dry run of some kind so that they can spot potential weaknesses. Always assume that any individual who wants to pose a threat will do their homework beforehand.

Technology

Let's use metal detectors as an example. If you are concerned about people entering your facility with a firearm or knife, installing metal detectors will serve as an extra layer of security operated as intended. Faulty or outdated technology is essentially junk that is only there to present an illusion of security.

Security cameras are notorious for this. So many facilities "install" them but don't hook them up to a monitoring and recording system. In the cases in which they *are* hooked up to a system, the facility might not check that they are adequately maintained or repaired as needed.

If all you want is a security tool that can "deter" potential threats just by being seen, you might as well put up a scarecrow.

Depending who you ask, some would say that "dummy" security cameras help with deterrence. I would argue this practice may expose the organization or business to legal and financial liability. If the leadership knows there is a potential for security risks, and they willingly install a dummy security feature, they could be opening the door to much larger issues down the road. The leadership has a fiduciary duty to protect people and property. They must never cut corners to create a false sense of security.

Take the murder of University of Utah student Mackenzie Lueck, for example. When she went missing on June 17, 2019, investigators stated that "the cameras could not have captured any evidence of her disappearance." This is because the cameras, which were located at the last known spot in which Lueck was known to be, did not record at all. (Moser, 2019) and (CBS News, 2019)

A Word on Technology vs. Preparation

Let's discuss technology a little further. It sometimes feels like we've made a century's worth of technological progress all within the last couple of decades, doesn't it? Security tools are, without a doubt, incredibly crucial. But there is a flip side to this, in that technological capabilities can instill a kind of "set-it-and-forget-it" mentality. Some people can be lulled into thinking that technology will essentially do most of the work for them.

Those who subscribe to that line of logic are in for a rude awakening if an incident should arise. Security equipment is not a replacement for your vigilance. Tools are only part of the equation. The safety of your facility is not something that can be fully automated.

Access Control

Balancing business operations with safety and security measures can prove to be a challenge. But finding a reasonable medium ground that does not risk the impact to your assets is crucial. Property, staff, and sensitive data are all company assets that must be kept safe and secure.

People should be vetted before entering a facility, if necessary. Vendors, visitors, customers, employees, and anyone else who intends to enter the premises should always go through the same access control process. Not doing so shows signs of complacency and vulnerability. Rosters, identification cards, badge exchange processes, and personnel escorts strengthen the security of a facility and show potential threats that you and your personnel view physical safety as a high priority.

Human Resource departments should work in conjunction with security departments to strategically rollout a system such as the aforementioned I.D. cards. These cards should be unique, hard to duplicate and provide visually identifiable information. An organizational visitor policy should also be introduced and enforced. This act of vigilance will provide another layer of safety to reduce the capability of a bad actor from bringing in weapons or harmful devices.

Escort

Uncontrolled movement is a vulnerability that puts many businesses and organizations at risk. All visitors should be accompanied throughout the facility by an escort to reduce the probability of espionage, vandalism, or theft. This practice should be rolled into the organizational visitor policy mentioned above. It creates another layer of security to protect the sensitive nature of your internal operations and restricted areas. In my security walkthroughs, I have witnessed contractors working independently within facilities during normal business hours as well as after hours. What's to say these individuals are not secretly collecting sensitive information for competitors, or even planting hazardous items that may harm people at a later point in time?

Safety Protocol

As part of your organizational visitor policy, implementation of an electronic visitor record is a highly beneficial strategy. These systems track who is entering your facility and can provide the visitor with your respective safety rules and security practices.

I was particularly impressed with one of the client sites I recently visited. Upon entering a vestibule, I was immediately directed to an iPad outlining the facility's safety expectations and restrictions. I was then instructed to sign their organizational visitor logbook. Once I did, I received an electronic version of what I had signed. This simple but highly proactive step serves as a warning for any visitor that may have bad intentions, as well as physically enforces a sense of safety and security with their employees.

2

The Equation

"Knowing is not enough. We must apply. Willing is not enough. We must do."

Bruce Lee

When you begin to seriously think of proactive behavior and what it entails, you soon realize that it can be a very complex notion. But when you boil it down, it is about managing uncertainty to the best of your ability. It is also knowing what to do with the information or resources you have at your disposal in order to manage that uncertainty. People that are proactive may have a combination of the following ten characteristics:

Ten Characteristics of Proactive People

1. They are empowered to make a choice.
2. They plan for the future, so they are prepared to act before they are in danger.
3. They consider possible scenarios and anticipate what may happen before it happens.
4. They keep an organized list of some kind.

5. They take the initiative, identify, and analyze risks while staying aware of their respective consequences.

6. They are engaged and have a mental picture of how to solve a problem (a response roadmap).

7. They have the foresight and are able to anticipate situations (danger, incidents, crisis) before they occur.

8. They rehearse preventative measures.

9. They act and do not procrastinate.

10. They hold themselves accountable.

After reviewing this list, how many of these can you relate to? If your answer is few, if any, then you have an opportunity to sharpen up your proactive skill sets.

The dictionary definition of "proactive" was cited earlier in this book, nevertheless, a concept such as this can have a sort of abstract meaning, one with subtle differences in interpretation from person to person. This list of characteristics provides an insight into how you can make a change today to be truly proactive. The common thread you'll notice in that list is that proactive individuals take the initiative and do not wait for others to guide them in their decision-making process. This is a skill that can be developed through continuous practice by approaching and analyzing a diverse set of situations with a proactive state of mind.

Obviously, you can't predict what is going to happen in your day to day activities. But if you prepare and have the appropriate mindset, you will be in a better position to manage the uncertainty. Keep in mind that preparedness is not only applicable to crisis management situations. Life always requires you to have a certain level of preparedness. The motto "Be Prepared" isn't strictly for the Boy Scouts, after all.

Think about when you are preparing to travel overseas or across the country. You arrange your clothes based on the destination you will visit, arrange your toiletries according to the number of days you will be traveling, and take the necessary steps to manage your finances in advance. This is an excellent example of preparation in relation to a future situation.

Another example of proactiveness can be seen in the work ethic of certain individuals. Some people wait to be told what to do and when to do it. They react to problems instead of staying ahead of issues. On the other hand, a proactive person seeks feedback and analyzes trends in the workplace instead of waiting for colleagues or customers to provide the information needed. When problems arise, they take the initiative and seek out a solution rather than wait for the situation to blow over. If foresight and initiative can get you ahead in your career, just think of what they can do for your everyday life.

The Proactiveness Equation

Being proactive is vital to the way you go about your day, especially as we head into the new decade. As I've stated before, a low level of proactiveness in any facet of our lives can be the greatest determinant to our safety and security, especially when we're at work with colleagues or at school with students and faculty.

To help in developing a proactive state of mind, I have created a conceptual and analytical equation that should aide you in instilling proactive behaviors. If followed correctly, it should help you evaluate what you need to do in order to stay one step ahead and identify any and all actionable ways in which you can further develop your own foresight.

This "Proactiveness Equation" has eleven variables to measure the proactive state of mind, with ten being in the numerator and one in the denominator. The equation itself is represented in Figure 2.1. Increasing the value of the factors in the numerator increases the value of proactiveness. Decreasing the value of the denominator — the totality of circumstances — decreases the value of proactiveness. This element is the most important variable in the proactiveness equation.

Always remember that a lack of self-awareness may render the entire equation to become useless. You must trust yourself throughout the process and understand that no matter how tough things get, you will be able to rise to the occasion and succeed in saving yourself and others with a positive mental attitude.

FIGURE 2.1: Proactiveness Equation

$$P^1 = \frac{(P^2 + C + P^3) * (P^4 + L + E^1 + E^2 + T) * (SA + DM)}{ToC}$$

PCP (Refer to Figure 2.2)
PLEET (Refer to Figure 2.3)

Where:
P^1 = Proactive
P^2 = Perception
C = Comprehension
P^3 = Projection
P^4 = People
L = Location
E^1 = Event
E^2 = Environment
T = Time
SA = Self-Awareness
DM = Decision Making
ToC = Totality of Circumstances

Each component of this equation is somewhat non-circumstantial when looked at individually. But when you take a step back and analyze the big picture, together, they create a total package that can reinforce your proactive mindset.

$P^2 + C + P^3$

1. *Perception*

Perception rates how effectively you gather data within your current situation, location, and environment. For example, do you perceive your current environment as normal or aggressive? Are you making sure you're aware of people's behaviors and mannerisms? Does anything seem abnormal? Listen to your intuition. What does it tell you?

2. *Comprehension*

Do you perceive a threat, or do you feel safe? This question can be answered by using your accurate interpretation of the data you have accumulated upon analyzing your environmental factors.

3. *Projection*

Now combine perception and comprehension. Based on the result you get, what do you anticipate will happen? Try to practice by developing a potential scenario in your mind, and be sure to mentally map out an exit plan or a reactive strategy.

$$\mathbf{P}^4 + \mathbf{L} + \mathbf{E}^1 + \mathbf{E}^2 + \mathbf{T}$$

4. *People*

Be aware of people's clothing, their actions, and overall demeanor. For example, clothing that is counter to the current weather conditions, such as a trench coat in the summer, should be seen as a red flag. Another example might be something like a person wearing military or tactical gear in a mall or other business area.

5. *Location*

Understanding how individuals act within their culture is of vital importance. When you are educated and aware of cultural intricacies, diversity, and norms as they relate to how people of different cultures interact with each other, it will help you either identify or dismiss a potential threat.

6. *Event*

Each location has its own environmental factors. In this context, the "environment" refers to all the dynamics at a current location, such as security, crime, or even weather. Understanding the respective environmental factors could help you identify or dismiss a threat.

7. *Environment*

Having an initial understanding of the venue you are visiting will help you develop awareness in terms of what type of activity and etiquette is typical of the setting. For instance, loud noises and aggressive behaviors might be typical at a sports stadium, but not at a library.

8. *Time*

The time of day, year, or season can alter the security factors of a particular environment. It is important to understand the different dynamics during these times, as doing so can help you identify or dismiss a threat. As an example, the U.S. Secret Service identified active shooter attacks occurred "in every month except December and occurred on every day of the week. Over half of the incidents took place between the hours of 7:00 a.m. and 3:00 p.m." (U.S. Secret Service, 2019)

This information alone can help you remain aware from a statistical framework.

SA + DM

9. *Self-Awareness*

This step pertains to how clearly you know your strengths, weaknesses, fears, and capability to react to your environment's changes while you are under pressure. Stay cognizant of your surroundings and remain conscious of any risks that may exist. Understanding how you manage anxiety and stress is also a key aspect of self-awareness. All this will add up and strengthen your ability to make good decisions.

10. Decision Making

"In practice, safe decision making depends on the continuous extraction of technical and environmental information, as well as the integration of knowledge to form a coherent mental picture that will help direct perception and anticipate future events." (Dominguez, 1994) This boils down to how you process the information you've gathered and how to select which option to take.

ToC

11. Totality of Circumstances

"Totality of Circumstances" fully develops once all the factors you are aware of are analyzed through the lens of all the information you have gathered in your training. Remember, each of these factors won't mean much on their own, but the sum of all their parts combined gives you an overall picture that covers most every aspect of a potential threat.

A Closer Look at PCP

Dr. Mica R. Endsley has led the field of situational awareness with her groundbreaking research. Dr. Endsley's three levels of situational awareness, the aforementioned "PCP" (Perception, Comprehension, and Projection) provide a tangible framework that enables our understanding through its applicability within our lives. (Endsley, 1995) The phases of PCP are shown in Figure 2.2.

FIGURE 2.2: PCP Graphic

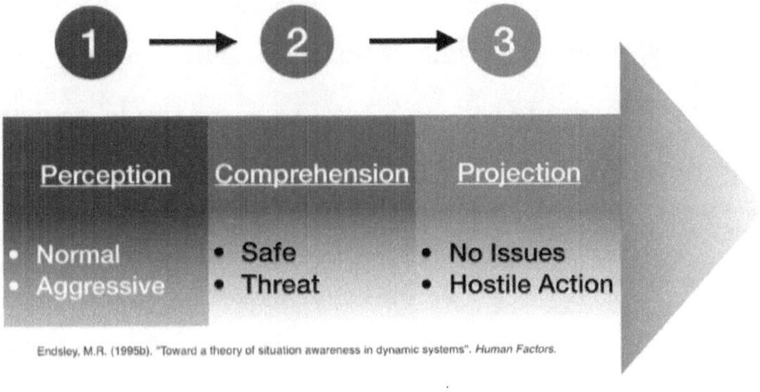

Endsley, M.R. (1995b). "Toward a theory of situation awareness in dynamic systems". *Human Factors.*

Perception

When you're entering any environment, or even if you're already present in said environment, you naturally collect bits of surrounding data. This data can present itself as auditory or visual. As an example, you may be near enough to a person or people to eavesdrop on their conversation and listen for potential threats. Maybe you see something suspicious like an abandoned gym bag in a public area. The data can even present itself in the olfactory sense, as in something that you can smell, like a gas leak. This data, combined with your intuition, will help you sense whether the environment is normal or if it is possibly aggressive.

Comprehension

This building block of intuition leads to understanding your current situation and applying that data into your pre-established mental model. Your personal experiences with sensing danger at earlier points in your life will enable your mental model to determine whether you feel safe or feel a threat. Think of it as remembering your past to recognize your present so that you may predict your future.

Projection

As mentioned before, environmental factors play a significant role in anticipating danger. Those of us who play chess, even casually, know that we must anticipate the big picture and not just the current move. So how do you stay sharp and ahead of the danger? You go out and live your life. The more you expose yourself to diverse scenarios, the better you'll be at projecting what may happen in the future. I'm certainly not suggesting that you seek out dangerous situations and willfully throw yourself into them. You can mentally expose yourself to these scenarios in your everyday life, which will help train your mind to perceive the possibilities for danger within any environment. Practicing this regularly is one of the many crucial steps in the development of your mental model.

Let's look at a line of work in which strict protocols can be the difference between life and death: Aviation. Professional pilots have a rock-solid checklist they must adhere to before takeoff, and it makes for a great example of advanced situational awareness. They must always be aware of the variables within their surroundings before, during, and even after the flight. Each element on that pre-flight checklist (airplane inspection, manifesto, communication with air traffic control) has been vetted through years of risks faced by other pilots. Recognition of past mistakes came together one by one, and they eventually were assembled into the protocols that pilots use today.

It should also be noted that the process never has a finish line. The pilots of today certainly know a great deal more than the pilots of yesterday, but that doesn't mean they aren't keeping their minds open for the dangers that have yet to be recognized. Never assume that the knowledge you've accumulated is all the knowledge there is.

Once the pilot has gone through their checklist, and the plane is in the air, they must also understand each component within the diverse systems and processes they are managing through the flight. This includes the GPS systems, airplane sensors, troubleshooting protocols, and weather patterns, to name a few. Without this level of situational awareness, the lives of the plane's passengers and crew are in jeopardy. Having a proactive and prevention-focused approach will ensure a pilot is situationally aware, and that their aircraft, passengers, and crew are safe. There may be an autopilot setting for the plane itself, but it's safe to assume that any would-be pilot who thought that the autopilot setting is a fair replacement for their situational awareness never made it out of flight school.

Let's take this pilot analogy and bring it back to ground level so that we may better understand how it applies to our everyday world. Consider the risks, damage, and trauma that could be unleashed if we were not situationally aware while in a public setting. Of course, those who find themselves in such a situation are never fully prepared, but by employing awareness, the ability to mitigate risks may increase the odds of survival.

Allowing yourself to become proactive is, without a doubt, the first step in allowing yourself to become reactive. The sooner you're able to recognize a threat, the better your response to it will be, and you'll be in a better position to manage uncertain situations.

A Closer Look at PLEET

The increased complexity of life has amplified the need to understand the societal pressures we face on a daily basis. Although PCP is a great framework to understand situational awareness, it alone may not be enough. We must utilize the contemporary factors and variables and combine them with the PCP process to help make effective decisions. All three levels have to be magnified by including the environmental factors I had mentioned earlier.

So ask yourself, what are the environmental factors that you must pay attention to?

In my own experience, there are five of these in total: people, location, environment, event, and time (see Figure 2.3).

FIGURE 2.3: PLEET Graphic

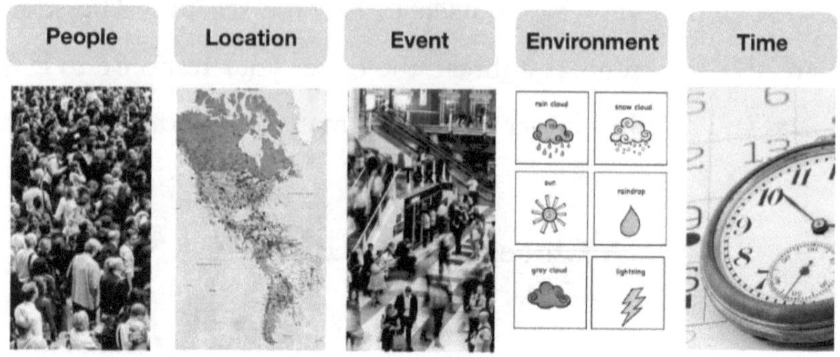

1. *People:*

Here you're closely monitoring such details as a person's attire, accessories, demeanor, and actions. Perhaps you are listening to conversations being held on a telephone by nearby people, or between people who are speaking one on one. In some instances, you might even be listening in on the conversations a person might be having with themselves.

Have a look at their appearance. This doesn't mean you should profile. Certain types of religious garb or "urban" clothing are *not* necessarily indicators of an individual with violent intentions. Instead, notice if they are wearing clothing that doesn't apply to the current weather conditions, such as a long trench coat in the summertime or combat gear inside of a business establishment, parking lot, or any other public area.

In terms of behavior, are they acting suspicious? Do they have an aggressive demeanor? If you answered yes to any of these indicators, this person may be a potential threat and should be observed closely. (Please refer to the sections titled "Warning Signs and Potential Threat Indicators" for further explanation.)

Here's an example: an individual wearing combat gear is stepping out of the driver side of their vehicle before proceeding towards the trunk of their car. Once they open the trunk, they pull out a large bag and walk aggressively towards a facility such as a school or business. If you're not aware enough to spot all those red flags, you might want to seriously think about why something like that doesn't seem out of the ordinary to you.

2. *Location:*

Understanding how individuals act within their culture is of vital importance. Being aware of their cultural intricacies and norms can help you identify or dismiss a potential threat. Do you hear people talking loudly amongst each other? Do people talk with their hands and discuss topics very close to each other? Being aware of these things can help keep you from jumping to conclusions.

Bear in mind that we live in a diverse and globalized society, and people should not be judged on their mannerisms alone.

Consider analyzing how the majority of the people within that setting are interacting with each other and then attempt to isolate a particular person's actions if they should stand out. Take the example of the Sri Lanka bombing mentioned earlier in this book. People listening to prayers were standing calm and patient outside of the mosque. The perpetrator walked briskly past everybody with an apparent level of intent. This behavior definitely stuck out. (Global News , 2019)

But what about an example that's a little more domestic? Ask yourself, is American behavior totally consistent within all fifty states? Technically, no. For instance, there are certain states within the United States of America that have liberal gun laws. In these States, it is not uncommon to see a rifle on a rack in the back of trucks or for individuals to open-carry their firearms in public. Arizona, Alaska, Wyoming, Vermont, Kansas, Kentucky, Mississippi, Utah, Missouri are some such states.

On the other hand, if an individual open carry their firearm into a public setting in states such as California, Connecticut, Colorado, Maryland, Massachusetts, New Jersey, New York, or the District of Columbia, that may raise some alarms since those states have far stricter gun laws.

3. *Event*

Understanding your setting will help you develop an awareness of what type of activity is generally known or accepted etiquette. Sights and sounds should be observed, and if they don't seem to fit the normal activity that's typical of that location, they could be determined as a threat.

Let's say it's Independence Day and you're watching a firework show. Would it be uncommon to hear loud popping sounds? Of course not. What about if you're in a car dealership service area? You'd probably hear some intermittent loud noises, wouldn't you? These noises would not be out of the ordinary, and therefore would most likely not register as a threat.

On the other hand, if you hear the sounds of "firecrackers" and people yelling or screaming inside a business, school, or church, these sounds would be atypical in relation to the setting. Obviously, you would register these sounds as potential threats.

4. *Environment:*

Each location has its own environmental intricacies. These can be anything from security presence to weather conditions.

Understanding these environmental factors could help you identify or dismiss a threat.

For example, statistics show that the threat of being kidnapped in certain parts of the world is severe. On April 9, 2019, the U.S. Department of State issued a travel advisory warning for countries with the highest threat of kidnapping. Afghanistan, Central African Republic, Iran, and Venezuela are a few out of the 35 countries they outlined. (U.S. Department of State, 2019) On the other hand, the likelihood of being kidnapped in a city like San Francisco is not nearly as severe. By knowing this, you can adjust your level of awareness accordingly.

5. Time:

The time of day, year, or season can impact the security environment. It is important to understand the different dynamics during these times to help identify or dismiss a threat.

Let's say you are traveling through a "rough" neighborhood in Chicago at 11:00 a.m. Would your awareness be heightened if you were traveling through that same neighborhood at 11:00 p.m.? Absolutely.

If you're looking for an international example, let's use Brazil. When you're traveling through tourist areas in Brazil during the times of the year in which tourism is slow, this may not cause an elevated state of awareness. But if you're traveling during their Carnival do Brasil festival, that should cause a heightened state of alertness because violent perpetrators are known to prey on tourists during this season.

A Closer Look at Totality of Circumstances

Now that we've gone over PCP and PLEET let me take a moment to reiterate how vital the totality of circumstances framework and should be taken seriously. Remember, not one single factor alone will determine an active shooter. You must gather all the facts that are available to you at that time and add them up as a whole to determine whether or not the threat is credible.

As you mentally strengthen your vigilance, you're going to inevitably bring your awareness to many variables. It might feel like too much all at once, but you must not allow yourself to become overwhelmed.

Remember, no one variable will determine or negate the probability of an active shooter threat. You must consider all the information and factors available at that point in time to predict as accurately as possible whether a threat is credible or not.

3

Key Characteristics

"Human behavior flows from three main sources: desire, emotion, and knowledge."

Plato

Warning Signs

Potential active shooters don't just fall out of the sky. But at the same time, they aren't wearing signs around their necks either. If you're trying to identify one before they take any violent action, you'll find that there are no black-and-white answers. There are only warning signs.

We've already gone over warning signs on one level, so now let's take a look at another. Knowing and understanding the general behavior of people is key to when attempting to identify these potential warning signs. Observable pre-attack behaviors, if recognized early, could disrupt whatever plans they might have. According to the United States Secret Service, 78% of perpetrators exhibit warning signs before pre-attack planning. (U.S. Secret Service, 2019)

Figure 3.1 depicts what I call the "Change in Behavior Doom Loop." The elements inside each bucket reflect concerning behaviors that could help stop or prevent a potential attack. These behaviors may be published and reflected on social media or other mediums. Again, you must consider the totality of circumstances before making any judgment on a person or group of individuals.

FIGURE 3.1: Change in Behavior Doom Loop

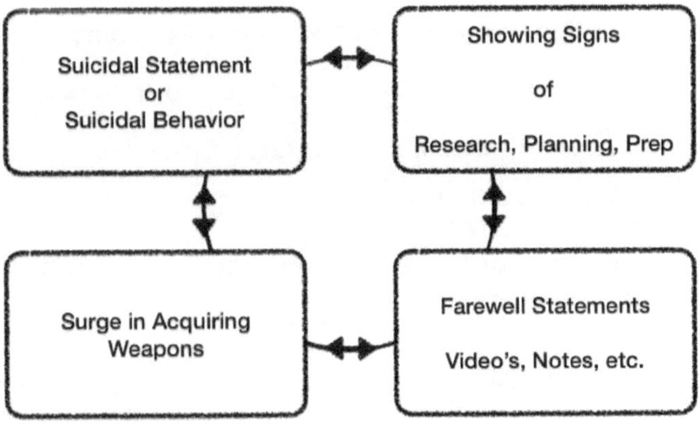

1. **Suicidal Statement or Suicidal Behavior**

Is the individual making statements or displaying behaviors which seem to indicate suicidal ideation, end of life planning, or an interest in destructiveness toward the world at large?

2. Showing Signs of Research, Planning, Preparation

Is the individual showing signs of research, planning, or preparation in terms of causing any violent acts?

Perhaps they are studying past shooter incidents and mentioning statistics. A sudden and apparent interest in this subject is a major red flag.

3. A Surge in Acquiring Weapons

Has the individual recently acquired weapons, ammunition, personal protective gear, tactical clothing, or other items? Have they engaged in a recent escalation of target practice and weapons training? Granted, this behavior may not be outside the norm for firearm enthusiasts, but it may also be something to watch out for. However, if the individual's interest in such things is considered to be somewhat sudden and outside of their character, that should be seen as a clearer warning sign.

4. Farewell Statements, Videos, Notes, Etc.

Has the individual prepared a "statement" or farewell writings? These may include manifestos, videos, notes, internet blogs, or emails. These statements may also be published on social media.

Personal Risk Factor Characteristics

Consider combining the following ten risk factor characteristics and the 14 behaviors that elicited concern with the previously mentioned warning signs "doom loop" so that you can predict as accurately as possible whether or not a threat is credible.

Ten Risk Factor Characteristics

1. History of substance abuse
2. Specific and direct threats
3. Past conflicts of violence with coworkers
4. Preoccupation with violence
5. Prior convictions for violent crime
6. Difficulty with anger management
7. Increased belligerence or hypersensitivity to criticism
8. Extreme disorganization
9. Homicidal or suicidal comments or threats
10. Any other noticeable changes in behavior

According to the U.S. Secret Service, several other behaviors elicited concern amongst family members, friends, work associates, community members, or social media followers. (U.S. Secret Service, 2019) The majority of the perpetrators in their report "exhibited behaviors that caused concerns in others," all of which are listed below.

14 Behaviors that Elicited Concern, U.S. Secret Service

1. Social media posts with alarming content
2. Escalating anger or aggressive behavior
3. Changes in behavior and appearance
4. Expressions of suicidal ideations
5. Writing about violence or weapons
6. Cutting off communications
7. Inappropriate behavior toward the opposite gender
8. Stalking and harassing behaviors
9. Increased depression
10. Increased drug use
11. Erratic behavior
12. Purchasing weapons
13. Threats of domestic violence
14. Acting paranoid

Threat Indicators

Some of these factors may be difficult to identify. After all, you can't be sure of what a person is thinking. It is human nature to keep many of our thoughts to ourselves. This is especially true of people with bad intentions. More often than not, they tend to hide the signs very well so as not to disrupt any plans they may be developing.

But there comes a time in which their thinking and intentions lead to observable behaviors that cannot easily be concealed. Based on the following five observable imminent threat indicators, we can start to see a larger picture, one that sheds more light on any possible threat. These five imminent threat indicators are apparel, actions, demeanor, eyes, and body language (see Figure 3.2).

FIGURE 3.2: Five Imminent Threat Indicators

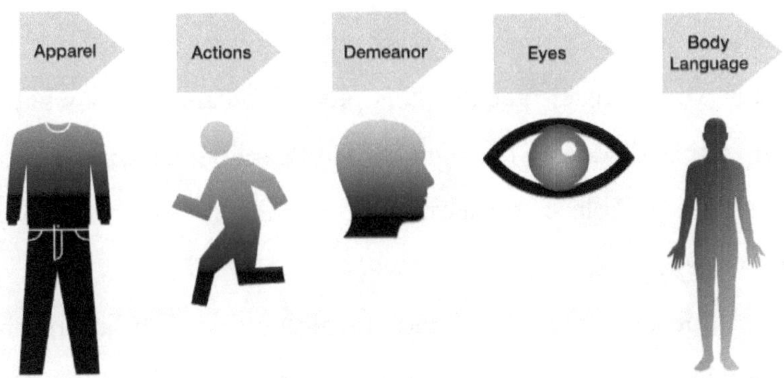

There are certain elements we can observe that are controllable. When you are observing someone, you can obviously see the clothing they are wearing and how they are positioning their body. These are all controllable behaviors for the individual.

Take for example, if the person is wearing an oversized coat or tactical gear, or keeping their hands in their pockets, or perhaps adjusting their clothing. The oversized coat may be used to hide a weapon. The tactical gear may be intended for carrying their ammunition. The hands in the pocket may also be used to conceal a weapon. The adjustment of the clothing may be to maintain the weapon's concealment.

On the other hand, there are certain physiological changes seen in an individual's behavior and body language that are non-controllable. Apparent, visible fear is just a component of how our body naturally manages itself for survival. Your breathing rate increases, your heart rate increases, your blood vessels constrict or dilate around the organs, and your muscles get a rich dose of blood to allow you to react quickly. This physiological effect is what goes on in your body during the fight or flight experience, and these signs may also be visible in someone who is willing themselves to carry out a violent act.

For example, if an individual with violent intentions is walking into a building in which they are unfamiliar with the layout, they may be visibly nervous or perhaps even terrified. This unfamiliarity can also manifest itself as indecisiveness, which may compel the individual to walk in and out of the area numerous times. If they suddenly decide they are not adequately prepared to follow through with their plan, they may show other signs of mental discomfort. They may exhibit what we've come to know as the "thousand-yard stare," a term that describes the faraway look that an individual may show when they start to detach from the world around them mentally. Their nervous behavior may also inhibit their ability to communicate effectively, which can cause the individual to stutter or pause between words.

To sum up, these imminent threat indicators break down to the following:

1. Apparel

- Apparel that is counter to the weather conditions (Long or bulky coat in the summer or tactical gear, for example)
- Apparel that is unusual for the setting (Such as combat fatigues with tactical gear in a shopping mall)
- Apparel that may help conceal their identity (Such as masks)

2. Actions

- Actions that seem odd or out of place
- Continuous touching around the waistband or pockets
- Loitering with no real purpose
- Aggressively pacing back and forth
- Displaying of any other overt physical actions

3. Demeanor

- Atypical body language
- Nervousness
- Sweating
- Shaking
- General unease
- Clenched jaw
- Noticeable physical discomfort
- "Thousand-yard stare"
- Indecisiveness
- Difficulty in communicating
- Noticeable unfamiliarity with surroundings

4. Eyes

- Angrily staring into the distance

- Hyper-vigilance

- Aggressive observation

- Shiftiness

5. Body Language

- Covert physical actions, trying to stay inconspicuous

- Stiff body language

- Hands in pockets

- Arms crossed

- Furtive movements towards waistband or bag, if they're carrying one

- Aggressive hand gestures

- Removing a gun from a waistband or bag

- Arms flailing

- Aggressive stance

Also, make a note of these two specific imminent threat indicators:

a. Voice

- Screaming at the top of their lungs
- Anger and intensity in their voice

b. Hands

- Hands can pull a trigger

- Hands can strike or choke

- Hands can pull a knife

- Without their hands, the perpetrator cannot carry out the plan.

Contemporary Threats

If you do not pay attention to the pre-attack warning signs, then threats can become a reality. Threats should be taken very seriously and reported immediately so that they may be investigated. You might think it all could amount to a possible waste of time, but it's better to waste time investigating a situation that turns out to be nothing than experience a tragedy.

If an individual makes verbal statements that could incite panic, that is not a laughing matter and should not be taken lightly. In fact, someone who thinks they are only joking about such things is running the risk of being prosecuted by law enforcement. Justice Oliver Wendell Holmes Jr. argued in *Schenck v. United States*, "The most stringent protection of free speech would not protect a man in falsely shouting 'fire' in a theatre and causing a panic." (Schenck v. United States, 1917)

It's better to be safe than to have regrets. The U.S. Secret Service has documented that "nearly all perpetrators (93%) have made threatening or concerning communications and more than three-quarters elicited concern from others prior to carrying out their attacks." (U.S. Secret Service, 2019) The moment a person voices their intentions to harm others, even if the comments are documented on social media, in blog posts, or during online gaming, they must be communicated. This can help mitigate the potential of the comment escalating to a tragedy.

Unfortunately, previous criminal incidents conducted by others may influence a person to put into motion any violent acts they may have previously been considering. These are known as copycats. As of this writing, nearly 26 people have been arrested since the El Paso and Dayton shootings due to the threats they have personally made which mirrored those two incidents. Here are those 26 episodes:

1. **August 4, 2019:** A Florida man called a Walmart located 10 miles south of Tampa and told an employee he was minutes away from shooting up the store, according to the Hillsborough County Sheriff's Office. The man now faces a false threat charge. (Halaschak, 2019)

2. **August 7, 2019:** A Texas Walmart had to be evacuated after a 13-year-old boy posted a threat on social media. Police in the town of Weslaco arrested the teen and charged him with making a terrorist threat. The boy's mother personally brought him to the police station. Her actions serve as an example that the warning signs should always be taken seriously, even when it comes to your loved ones. (The Monitor, 2019)

3. **August 8, 2019:** A man was accused of walking into a Missouri Walmart wearing body armor and carrying a handgun and rifle less than a week after a gunman killed 22 people in a Texas Walmart. He **said it was a "social experiment"** and claimed he did not intend to cause panic. As you can imagine, his weak excuse didn't stop police from

charging the man with making a terrorist threat. (Boyette, 2019)

4. **August 9, 2019:** A 23-year-old Las Vegas man was charged with possession of destructive devices after authorities found bomb-making materials in his home. The FBI says he was planning to attack a synagogue and a gay bar. (U.S. Attorney's Office District of Nevada, 2019)

5. **August 9, 2019:** A 26-year-old man in Winter Park, Florida was arrested after investigators said he posted a threat on Facebook. The threat stated, "3 more days of probation left then I get my AR-15 back. Don't go to Walmart next week." (Karanth, Florida Man Arrested For Threatening To Shoot Up Walmart After El Paso Massacre , 2019)

6. **August 10, 2019:** Police in the town of Harlingen, Texas responded to a threat that a man posted on social media. The post read, "Harlingen Walmart will be shot up on August 11th." (Garcia, 2019) He was arrested at his home on charges of making a terrorist threat. (Harlingen Police Department, 2019)

7. **August 11, 2019:** A Palm Beach County, Florida mother, was accused of threatening to carry out a shooting at an elementary school. She was not happy that her children were being transferred there and felt that violent action would be

an appropriate response. The 28-year-old woman was charged with sending a written threat on Facebook to commit bodily injury. The message read, "I'm thinking of doing a school shooting at Barton." (WPTV Webteam , 2019)

8. **August 11, 2019:** A Mississippi teen was accused of posting threats on Facebook in which he stated his intentions to commit violent acts toward the Lamar County School District. The post had a picture of a weapon with a threat towards Oak Grove High School. (Burnett, 2019)

9. **August 12, 2019:** Authorities charged an 18-year-old Ohio man who the FBI says **threatened to assault federal law enforcement officers.** He expressed support for mass shooters in an online post which read, "in conclusion, shoot every federal agent on sight," and court documents say that the teen had a stockpile of weapons and ammunition. (Alsup, 2019)

10. **August 12, 2019:** A 25-year-old man from Jefferson County, West Virginia was arrested on charges of making terrorist threats online. The threat claimed, "he was a ticking time bomb that had already been diffused, was going to kill people, and was going to hurt people." (Ta, 2019)

11. **August 13, 2019:** Albert Lea Police arrested and charged a 15-year-old Minnesota girl for threatening to "shoot up" Albert Lea High School on her social media page. (Kamal, 2019)

12. **August 13, 2019:** A man was arrested in Phoenix, Arizona after police say he threatened to blow up an Army recruitment center. (azfamily.com News Staff, 2019)

13. **August 15, 2019:** A tip from a citizen, led Connecticut authorities and the FBI to investigate and arrest a man who made a Facebook post in which he openly expressed interest in committing a mass shooting. The man was in possession of weapons and tactical gear, the FBI and Norwalk Police Department said. (Holcombe, 2019)

14. **August 15, 2019:** A 15-year-old girl was arrested in Fresno, California for posting a photo of a Walmart gun case with rifles displayed and the caption "Don't come to school tomorrow," according to the city's police chief. She was charged with making terrorist threats. (ABC 30, 2019)

15. **August 16, 2019:** A 15-year-old boy was taken into police custody in Volusia County, Florida after investigators say he threatened to commit a school shooting in comments he made on a video game chat platform. The threat stated, "I Dalton Barnhart vow to bring my fathers m15 to school and

kill 7 people at a minimum." This incident serves as an example that even online gaming threats are taken seriously. (Sutton, 2019)

16. **August 16, 2019:** Two Mississippi juveniles were arrested in connection with threatening messages to two Tupelo schools. Their threats resulted in a school going into partial lockdown. (Carlisle, 2019)

17. **August 16, 2019:** A Florida man was arrested and charged with threatening to commit a mass shooting. His ex-girlfriend alerted authorities after the man sent her a serious of disturbing text messages. One text message read, "A good 100 kills would be nice." Another read, "A school is a weak target... id be more likely to open fire on a large crowd of people from over 3 miles away... I'd wanna break a world record for longest confirmed kill ever." (Nottingham, 2019)

18. **August 16, 2019:** A 14-year-old in Arizona was arrested by Tempe Police after he allegedly made online threats against a school. (abc15.com staff , 2019)

19. **August 16, 2019:** A 19-year-old Chicago man was arrested after police say he threatened to kill people at a women's reproductive health clinic on an online forum. A post on iFunny read, "I am done with my state and thier (sic) bullsh*t abortion laws and allowing innocrnt (sic) kids to be

slaughtered for the so called 'womans (sic) right." (Darran Simon, 2019)

20. **August 16, 2019:** A 35-year-old Clarksburg, Maryland resident, was arrested in Seattle after being charged with threatening to "to injure and kill a South Florida resident and to kill all Hispanics in Miami and other places." (US Attorney's Office Southern District of Florida, 2019)

21. **August 17, 2019:** Police in New Middletown, Ohio arrested a self-described white nationalist who they say threatened to **shoot a Jewish community center.** The video threat tagged the Jewish Community Center of Youngstown on Instagram with a caption that read, "Police identified the Youngstown Jewish Family Community shooter as local white nationalist Seamus O'Rearedon." (Dakin Andone, 2019)

22. **August 18, 2019:** A man was arrested in Reed City, Michigan after authorities said he posted online videos making threats toward Ferris State University and several other locations. (FOX 17 NEWS, 2019)

23. **August 18, 2019:** Claremore, Oklahoma police arrested an 18-year-old who they say made social media threats against the families of police officers. (Baron, 2019)

24. **August 19, 2019:** A 38-year-old truck driver was arrested after making "credible threats to conduct a mass shooting

and suicide" according to a sworn affidavit filed in the Southern District of Alabama. (Martin, 2019)

25. **August 19, 2019:** Maui Police arrested an 18-year-old man after a social media post claimed he intended to "shoot up a school." (KITV Web Staff, 2019)

26. **August 19, 2019:** A 37-year-old Rapid City, South Dakota man, was arrested and charged with threatening to blow up state and federal government agencies. (KELOLAND News, 2019)

These 26 examples demonstrate several of the behaviors cited by the U.S. Secret Service. The behaviors revealed by these individuals ranged from social media posts with alarming content from the perpetrators, changes in their behavior, aggressive behavior, threats of domestic violence, and erratic behavior. Fortunately, several alleged threats were stopped from escalating to a deadly incident because of the heroic determination from people who were concerned, or because the individual leaked their information on social media, amongst other methods.

Mental Muscle Memory

The term "in the zone" is often used by those who have a certain skill set that they developed with constant and repetitive practice. After a certain point, all that hard work and dedication add up to a substantial level of confidence that allows their skills to take over naturally. Skilled individuals, whether they're performers, athletes, artists, engineers or something in between, have often said that they have a sort of "out of body experience" during these moments. This term goes by many other names, but we'll call it "mental muscle memory."

Never forget that failure is an integral part of the development process. By investing long hours of practice, you let yourself become more and more exposed to opportunities for serious improvement. As is the case with any training process, you'll obviously face a number of challenges.

Learning how to remain situationally aware in relation to an active shooter incident is no different, and you'll encounter a unique set of obstacles as you move forward. The fear that these situations bring along with them is often immediate and with little to no warning at all. They're jarring and terrifying, which leads to disorientation and confusion.

As a result, those who find themselves in an incident can experience an out of body experience of an entirely different breed. They may lock up as opposed to flow through. This reaction is perfectly understandable, considering the extreme stress that has been thrust upon them. Even the most highly trained and highly decorated members of the military will tell you about the first harrowing seconds of a crisis they experienced, and how it took so much of their focus to ground themselves back into reality and get their bearings before it was too late. But as natural as this response may be, it will do you absolutely no good.

In order to achieve the out of body experience that keeps you and those around you safe and secure, you must develop a sense of muscle memory to your mind. This is absolutely crucial. Mental muscle memory and intuition make for an excellent partnership. As one gets stronger, the other gets sharper, just as the mind works in conjunction with the body.

Mental Muscle Memory Scenarios

How do you develop your mind's muscle memory? Practice makes perfect. You must rehearse the concept of identifying hazards and threats. Then you can test how you'll react to a certain scenario based on pre-set variables and conditions.

Let's test it out with several scenarios. Rehearse these either on paper, in your mind, or with colleagues and friends. What would you do in these make-believe scenarios?

Mental Muscle Memory Scenario #1

It is 7:00 a.m. on a pleasant Tuesday morning, and you are heading to work. You have a very important meeting to attend at 9:00 am. It usually takes you 45 minutes to commute to your office, but today traffic was heavier than usual. It delayed your commute by 20 minutes.

You are now frustrated, annoyed, and upset that your morning has not gone as you had planned. You decided to maximize your time by making a business phone call related to the upcoming sales meeting. At approximately 8:05 a.m., you park the vehicle on the second-floor parking lot of your office. As you exit the car, you continue your conversation with your phone pressed to the side of your face. You make your way to the first floor and walk towards the building.

It is now 8:15 a.m., and you are approaching the main entrance. Meanwhile, people have been waving at you to not go into the lobby for the past 20 seconds. They are also telling you to avoid the area. But you continue the conversation, perhaps denying what you're hearing, questioning their comments, or just thinking they are crazy. Or perhaps you may not hear them at all.

As you approach the turnstile and enter the lobby, you confront a perpetrator aiming a weapon at you. The perpetrator has already killed several people inside the lobby.

1. Could you have avoided the lobby?
2. What could you have done through the course of your walk from the car to the lobby?

Mental Muscle Memory Scenario #2

You are the Human Resources Vice President of a 29,000-square-foot warehouse manufacturing plant which employs 200 people. Your plant is well known for its industrial water valves around the world. You are responsible for your company's organizational development, recruitment, and staffing, amongst other duties.

As you arrive at the airport at 2:00 p.m., you realize you have 150 twitter messages, 8 missed voicemails, and one call is coming in. You decide to let it go to voicemail. As you go through the terminal, you start to look at the TVs displaying breaking news. The headline reads "Active Shooter in Valve Manufacturing Plant."

Your heart drops as you hope it's not your plant. As you continue to watch, you're floored by the realization that it is, in fact, your plant. You pick up the next call, and it is your Director of HR on the line to notify you about the incident. You are briefed that the incident lasted ninety minutes, with five people dead, including a police officer, and multiple wounded. The perpetrator is an employee the company fired the very same day.

Your Director of HR also notified you that the reports you and your team were supposed to read stated the perpetrator mentioned to another co-worker the morning of the shooting that if he was fired, he was going to kill every other employee and "blow police up."

Your director also told you they knew the former employee also carried a gun in his vehicle. This information was never funneled to you because the perpetrator always made "off the wall" statements, and no one ever thought he would take any violent actions.

The perpetrator was notoriously known to refuse wearing safety glasses and was written up many times because of his refusal to wear them. After a disciplinary meeting with the perpetrator, employees reported they saw him "walking over to his workstation to retrieve something."

According to these employee statements, he then put on a hoodie and went into the bathroom just before the meeting. When the manager told him he was fired, the perpetrator used profanity and then began firing.

1. Could you have established better protocols to help keep your employees safe?
2. What could you have done through the course of the employees' employment?
3. What training could you have offered your employees to ensure they remain safe?

Achieving a sense of Muscle Memory is not so much a goal as it is a result. As you go through this book and put what you've learned into practice, you'll find that the sense will become stronger.

The more you try to pursue it, the more you'll find that it's coming in your direction. You'll be surprised at how the process will meet you halfway.

4

Managing the Uncertainty

"It's a wicked world, and when a clever man turns his brain to crime it is the worst of all."

Arthur Conan Doyle

The New Norm

We are living in a new norm, it seems. Many people are afraid to enjoy their day-to-day public activities because of the constant threat of mass murders or active shooter incidents. Active shooter and mass murder incidents have become part of the society we currently live in within the United States of America.

From coast to coast, the frequency of active shooter incidents has increased exponentially over the years. No person, geographical location, business, private, or governmental organization is immune to these incidents. The impact on the public's perception of their city's safety as well as the credibility of an organization's security infrastructure may be on the line. They catch you off guard and by surprise, thus creating a level of uncertainty.

These incidents create fear, anxiety, worry, and terror amongst our communities, just as they are intended to do. This is especially true in school settings, from preschools all the way to universities.

Parents not only aim to provide their children with a top-notch education. They entrust school officials with the safety and security of our children as well. But in this day and age, is that truly possible?

Obviously, schools are not the only locations impacted by the threat of an active shooter or mass murder incident. Our current reality shows that any location, irrespective of its internal operations, yearly revenue, or global recognition may be impacted if the people are not proactively aware of its risks, hazards and physical security vulnerabilities. No business is immune.

For example, Google reportedly earned $136.8B in 2018, which is a 22% increase from 2017. (Inc., 2019) You would think a multi-billion dollar corporation would have had a robust security infrastructure to protect their assets and people, wouldn't you? But unfortunately, even their security protocol seems to have its limits.

For example, there was an incident on April 3, 2018 in which a perpetrator entered the YouTube headquarters and injured four people. (Gonzalez, 2018) This incident can serve as an example of how even the best available resources can come up short if not fully utilized. Constant vigilance, rigorous focus, and unwavering preparedness are always of optimal importance.

According to the FBI, commercial facilities are the most vulnerable areas facing a threat of active shooters. The FBI identified and segmented the locations into seven areas where other incidents occurred from 2000 through 2018 and will continue to face a threat as we head into the future.

These seven locations listed below are where the majority of the mass shooting incidents have occurred:

Seven Vulnerable Locations Facing a Threat of Active Shooters

1. Commercial Areas
    a. Businesses Open to the Public
    b. Businesses Closed to the Public
    c. Malls
2. Educational Environments
    a. Pre-kindergarten through 12th grade
    b. Institutions of higher learning

3. Open Space Locations

4. Health Care Facilities

5. Government Facilities

    a. Military

    b. Other government properties

6. Places of Worship

7. Residences

Throughout 2018 alone, there were 27 active shooter incidents which occurred in diverse locations throughout the United States, according to the FBI. (FBI, 2019) The largest concentration of the incidents occurred in places of commerce, with 16 out of the 27 incidents. Nine of those 16 incidents occurred in businesses open to the public. The remaining seven of those 16 incidents occurred in businesses closed to the public.

Five out of the 27 incidents occurred in academic locations. Four out of those five incidents were high schools, and one incident happened in a middle school. Two out of those 27 incidents occurred in open space areas. An additional 2 out of 27 incidents occurred in healthcare facilities. One out of the 27 incidents took place on government property, and the last incident occurred in a place of worship. (See Appendix B)

Diversity of Hazards

Unchecked hazards usually present themselves as eventual threats. A hazard is an unsafe condition that is dangerous and harmful, one which has the potential to cause injury, illness, or damage to people or property. Their typical categories are "natural" or "manmade." The hazard of an active shooter is obviously a manmade threat. It can also be known as "adversarial" or "human-caused." (There are three additional **hazard categories** you can reference in **Appendix A**.)

A "threat" is essentially an indication of a potential undesirable event. It refers to a situation or scenario in which a person could do something destructive. An example might be an attacker breaching private territory against a campus border, or a natural occurrence that could cause an undesirable outcome, such as a fire damaging a school's information technology hardware. A threat is created when a threat actor, which we'll refer to as a "bad actor," intentionally exploits a vulnerability.

There are six questions (see **Figure 4.1**) you can use as a guide to conduct a basic analysis of a potential threat so that you may prioritize the resources to mitigate risks, hazards, or vulnerabilities accordingly. Once you have identified a threat (listed on Appendix A), utilize this list to conduct a basic vulnerability assessment. You can also use this list while in public to analyze your immediate environment. I have provided a basic guide for the options associated with each topic.

FIGURE 4.1: Basic Threat Assessment

#	Topic	Question	Options
1	Threat	What is the threat?	See Appendix A
2	Probability or Frequency	How often will the threat or hazard occur?	a. Unlikely b. Likely c. Highly Likely
3	Magnitude	What is the extent of expected damage?	a. Negligible b. Limited c. Critical
4	Warning	How much time do you have to warn others?	a. Days b. Hours c. Seconds
5	Duration	How long will the threat last?	a. Days b. Hours c. Minutes
6	Priority	How critical is the threat? Based on the prior answers.	a. Low b. Medium c. High

The first step is to identify the threat itself. The second step is to determine the probability or frequency of occurrence. Use caution when determining all this. Not all threats will have a high likelihood of occurring. As an example, know that from a statistical perspective, a fire is much more likely to occur than an active shooter incident. However, the potential damage of both of those scenarios is critical. The available time you'll have in order to warn the right people could only be a few seconds. In a fire, it could take anywhere from days to control the damage or only minutes. But an active shooter ranges within seconds to hours. It all depends on how many variables are outside of your control, such as law enforcement presence. You will need to determine the priority of all these categories based on the chosen threat.

Diversity of Incidents

U.S. Government agencies have defined an active shooter as "an individual actively engaged in killing or attempting to kill people in a confined space or other populated area, generally with the use of a firearm." Furthermore, the term:

> "active shooter is used by law enforcement to describe a situation in which a shooting is in progress and an aspect of the crime may affect the protocols used in responding to and reacting at the scene of the incident. Unlike a defined crime, such as a murder or mass killing, the active aspect inherently implies that both law enforcement personnel and citizens have the potential to affect the outcome of the event based upon their responses." (Blair, 2014)

The term "mass murder" has generally been defined by the FBI as a multiple homicide incident in which four or more victims are murdered, within one event, and in one or more locations in close geographical proximity. Congress has defined "mass killings" as "three or more killings in a single incident." (United States Congress, 2019) Irrespective of which definition you use, it is appropriate to analyze the collective diversity of the facts.

FIGURE 4.2: Active Shooter Incident Locations - 2018

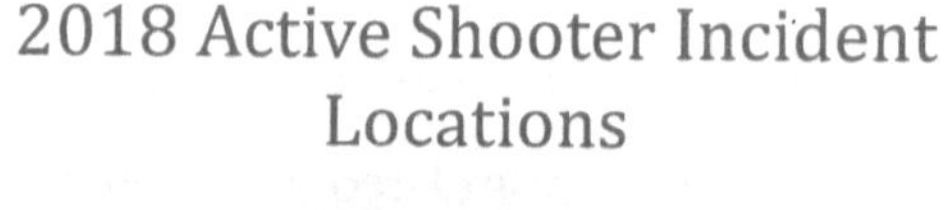

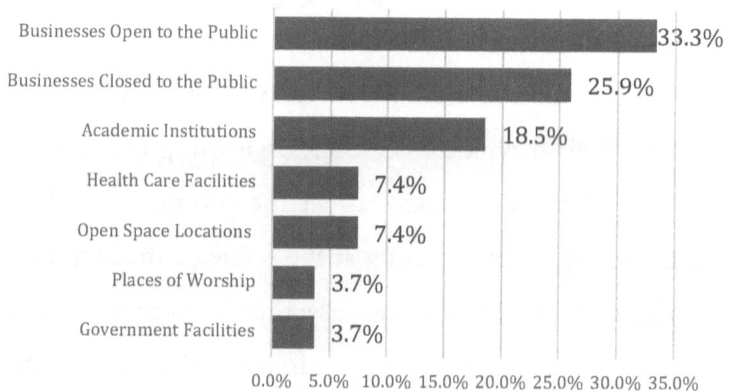

As I stated at the beginning of this chapter, the FBI concluded there were 27 episodes which classified as an active shooter incident throughout the year 2018 (see Figure 4.2). (U.S.

Department of Justice, 2019) The characteristics of these incidents are very diverse from a geographical and locational perspective. If we segment each incident by those perspectives, it may help us project and identify the areas that are at the highest risk.

33.3% of Active Shooter incidents occurred in Businesses Open to the Public

Be aware, from a statistical perspective, if you find yourself in a business area or inside of a business which is open to pedestrians, you are at a higher risk than other areas during an active shooter incident. Businesses open to the public typically do not have many access control security systems installed to restrict the flow of pedestrians. Obviously, they have security measures in place to detect theft and identify suspicious behavior. But their business model is highly dependable on the flow of people which puts this category at a higher risk. These locations range from bars, restaurants, banks, grocery stores, hotels, hospitals, etc. Here is a list of businesses open to the public that were impacted by an active shooter during 2018:

1. City Grill Café, March 7, 6:30 a.m. (Hurtsboro, Alabama)
2. Waffle House, April 22, 3:30 a.m. (Nashville, Tennessee)

3. Louie's Lakeside eatery, May 24, 6:30 p.m. (Oklahoma City, Oklahoma)

4. GLHF Game Bar, August 26, 1:34 p.m. (Jacksonville, Florida)

5. Fifth Third Center, September 6, 9:10 a.m. (Cincinnati, Ohio)

6. Kroger grocery store, October 24, 3:00 p.m. (Jeffersontown, Kentucky)

7. Hot Yoga Tallahassee, November 2, 5:37 p.m. (Tallahassee, Florida)

8. Borderline Bar and Grill, November 7, 11:20 p.m. (Thousand Oaks, California)

9. Motel 6, December 24, 2018, 11:00 a.m. (Albuquerque, New Mexico)

25.9% of Active Shooter incidents occurred in Businesses Closed to the Public

Businesses closed to the public are also at risk of an active shooter threat. These businesses typically have higher standards for their access control capabilities to restrict the flow of pedestrians. For example, if you are visiting a multinational company in the United States, there is a large chance you will have to show some form of identification, and you may have to either be buzzed or scanned into the building.

Either way, businesses in this category do not depend on the constant flow of customers. Therefore, they can restrict pedestrian traffic without hindering their daily operations. These locations range from multinational and international corporations, distribution centers, factories, and so forth.

Here is a list of businesses closed to the public that were impacted by an active shooter during 2018:

10. YouTube Headquarters, April 3, 12:45 p.m. (San Bruno, California)

11. Capital Gazette, June 29, 2:34 p.m. (Annapolis, Maryland)

12. T&T Trucking, Inc., September 12, 5:20 p.m. (Bakersfield, California)

13. WTS Paradigm, September 19, 10:30 a.m. (Middleton, Wisconsin)

14. Rite Aid Perryman Distribution Center's Liberty Support Center, September 20, 9:06 a.m. (Aberdeen, Maryland)

15. Ben E. Keith Gulf Coast, August 20, 2:00 a.m. (Missouri City, Texas)

16. Ben E. Keith Albuquerque, November 12, 6:56 p.m. (Albuquerque, New Mexico)

18.5% of Active Shooter incidents occurred in Academic Locations

The balance to educate students and maintain their safety through security measures should not be taken lightly. On some level or another, students across the country continue to fear that they may be the next target of an active shooter threat. As previously mentioned, these incidents occur within PK – 12 facilities as well as universities. None of these facilities are immune.

Here is a list of academic facilities which were impacted by an active shooter during 2018:

17. Marshall County High School, January 23, 7:57 a.m. (Benton, Kentucky)
18. Marjory Stoneman Douglas High School, February 14, 2:30 p.m. (Parkland, Florida)
19. Dixon High School, May 16, 8:00 a.m. (Dixon, Illinois)
20. Santa Fe High School, May 18, 7:30 a.m. (Santa Fe, Texas)
21. Noblesville West Middle School, May 25, 9:06 a.m. (Noblesville, Indiana)

7.4% of Active Shooter incidents occurred in Open Space Locations

Open spaces are essentially geographical locations that are located within highways, roads, streets, etc. Below is a list of open space locations impacted by an active shooter in the year 2018:

22. Highway 365 near Whitehall Road, May 4, 11:58 a.m. (Gainesville, Florida)
23. Highway 509 near Seattle-Tacoma International Airport, June 13, 1:42 p.m. (Seattle, Washington)

7.4% of Active Shooter incidents occurred in Health Care Facilities

Healthcare facilities certainly aren't immune to workplace violence. Below is a list of health care facilities impacted by an active shooter in 2018:

24. Helen Vine Recovery Center, November 5, 1:30 a.m. (San Rafael, California)
25. Mercy Hospital & Medical Center, November 19, 3:20 p.m. (Chicago, Illinois)

3.7% of Active Shooter incidents occurred in Government Facilities

Government facilities are typically on a heightened state of alert and on the lookout for suspicious activities or threats. This is especially true after the active shooter 2017 attack to Fort Lauderdale-Hollywood International Airport, the 2016 incident at Prince George's County Police Department District 3 Station incident, and the 2017 incident at Clovis-Carver Public Library incident. Below is the only government facility impacted by an active shooter during 2018.

26. Masontown Borough Municipal Center, September 19, 2:00 p.m. (Masontown, Pennsylvania)

3.7% of Active Shooter incidents occurred in Places of Worship

Following the 2015 incident at Emanuel African Methodist Episcopal Church in downtown Charleston, South Carolina, the 2017 First Baptist Church in Sutherland Springs, Texas, and the 2017 Burnette Chapel Church of Christ active shooter incidents, places of worship continue to also be on a heightened level of alert. Below is the only place of worship impacted by an active shooter during 2018.

27. Tree of Life Synagogue, October 27, 9:45 a.m. (Pittsburgh, Pennsylvania)

History of Incidents

As always, we must know our past to understand our future. Recognizing historical facts about these incidents may help understand the dynamics of our current societal crises. It may not help us predict future events entirely but having knowledge of past incidents is certainly useful. Studying how these incidents unfolded, who was involved, and how people and operations were impacted, is crucial. This will help set us on the right path to tackle this issue and possibly reduce or mitigate future incidents.

As noted by Dr. Vicki M. Abbinante in *Policy Decisions and Options-Based Responses to Active Shooters in Public Schools*, this phenomenon has existed and was documented before the United States of America was even a nation. The list below presents over a dozen historical examples of active shooters incidents in public schools. (Abbinante, 2017)

- In 1764, a Pennsylvania schoolhouse was attacked by a group of Native Americans. The attack resulted in one teacher being murdered, as well as a total of ten students. Only three students were left alive. (Rocque, 2012)

- In the following century, the United States would continue to see many shootings that involved students and teachers. However, none of these incidents included more than two victims and therefore, cannot be considered as mass shootings. (Ibid)

- It was not until 1927 in Bath Township, Michigan at the Bath School that people in this country would be shocked by the murders of 45 people accounting for 38 elementary-aged students and seven adults, with the use of both bombs and guns. (Ibid)

- In 1956, three teachers were shot in Maryland Park Junior High. (Ibid)

- In 1966, the country would witness the killing of 16 individuals on the campus of the University of Texas during a sniper shooting. This incident was one of the first to have a substantial amount of media coverage. (Lankford, 2013)

- In 1976, the California State University at Fullerton massacre took place, resulting in seven total deaths. (Ibid)

- On April 20th, 1999 in Littleton, Colorado, the Columbine High School shooting resulted in fifteen deaths. This incident is one of the first to bring awareness of a growing threat to the safety of students. (Ibid)

- In 2006, six students were killed at an Amish school in West Nickel Mines, Pennsylvania. (Ibid)

- In 2007, 33 were murdered at Virginia Tech University. (Kelly, 2012)

- In 2008, six students were shot dead at Northern Illinois University. (Ibid)

- In 2012, preschool students and teachers at Sandy Hook Elementary School in Newtown, Connecticut, were massacred. The total number of deaths was 26. (Ibid)

- In May of 2014, seven were gunned down by a fellow student on the campus of the University of California. (Ibid)

- In October of 2014, a shooting at Marysville Pilchuck High School in Washington resulted in five students being shot.(Kelly, 2012)

Active shooter or mass murder incidents are not a new phenomenon. They are essentially terrorist acts, which are as old as time. This particular list provided above shows a clear trend dating back before the year 1760 through 2014. Each incident was received with shock and surprise by the victims and people who experienced them.

So what exactly is an active shooter?

The Contemporary Active Shooter

Picture an active shooter in your mind. What do they look like? What distinctive features do they each share? If you are reading this while you are in public or amongst other people at work or school, casually look around you. Does anyone "look" like a potential active shooter?

I typically ask these questions during the *Proactive State of Mind Situational Awareness and Preparedness* (Ramirez, 2019) seminar training sessions I hold with my clients. The clients range from PK-12 grade school administrators, teachers, and staff, corporate executives, and employees. I let the questions linger, and I read the participant's body language to gauge their understanding of the matter at hand.

Nearly four out of five times, the response is consistent. "A shooter can be you, me, or anyone in this room," is an answer I heard during one of the sessions. "It can be anyone at work," is another example. "Any of our customers or vendors," is another example. "It is people like us," is another solid answer. With every response from the crowd, I typically ask them to elaborate on their answer. Again, the explanation is consistent with the research. The physical dynamics of perpetrators are diverse in cultural, sex, age, and class.

As mentioned earlier, the FBI defines an active shooter as "an individual actively engaged in killing or attempting to kill people in a confined space or other populated area, generally with the use of a firearm." The broadness of that definition goes to show how many demographics can fall within that definition.

The truth is, there is no way to profile these people with absolute certainty. Yes, the statistics clearly show that some demographics are more likely to carry out a mass shooting than others. But there are, and always will be, exceptions.

Let's have a closer look at ten active shooter incidents and see what stands out among these perpetrators:

1. San Jose, California

At approximately 6:00 a.m. on April 23, 2001, a 36-year-old Asian female, armed with a semi-automatic handgun, killed one person and wounded three others at the Laidlaw Education Services bus maintenance yard in San Jose, California. The perpetrator was arrested by law enforcement and charged with murder and attempted murder.

2. Blacksburg, Virginia

At approximately 7:15 a.m. on April 16, 2007, a 23-year-old Asian male, armed with two semi-automatic pistols, killed two people. At approximately 9:45 a.m., the perpetrator killed an additional 30 people and wounded 17 others at Virginia Tech in Blacksburg, Virginia. The perpetrator committed suicide after police breached the doors of the building where most of the shooting had taken place.

3. Washington, D.C.

At approximately 8:16 a.m. on September 16, 2013, a 34-year-old African American male, armed with a Remington Model 870 Express Synthetic Tactical 7-Round 12-gauge shotgun and a Beretta M9 9mm semi-automatic pistol, shot and killed 13 people and injured eight others at the Washington Navy Yard, Washington, D.C. At 9:25 a.m., the perpetrator was shot and killed by responding law enforcement officers.

4.   Orlando, Florida

At approximately 2:00 a.m. on June 12, 2016, a 29-year-old Middle Eastern male, armed with a Sig Sauer SIG MCX semi-automatic rifle and a 9mm Glock 17 handgun, killed 49 people and injured 53 others in the Pulse nightclub in Orlando, Florida. The perpetrator took hostages after police arrived and engaged in a gunfight with law enforcement. At approximately 5:00 a.m., police shot and killed the perpetrator.

5.   Fort Lauderdale, Florida

At approximately 12:54 p.m. on January 6, 2017. A 27-year-old Hispanic male was armed with a Walther PPS 9mm semi-automatic pistol with two magazines which he legally checked onto a flight from Alaska to Fort Lauderdale baggage locked in a secure container, his only checked baggage. He retrieved it in Fort Lauderdale and loaded the gun in the airport bathroom just before the attack. The perpetrator killed five and injured six. The perpetrator was apprehended by police.

6. Missouri City, Texas

At approximately 2:15 a.m. on August 20, 2017, a 29-year-old Latina female, armed with a semi-automatic weapon, killed two people and injured one person at the Ben E. Keith Warehouse located in Missouri City, Texas. The perpetrator fled and died of a gunshot wound.

7. Las Vegas, Nevada

At approximately 10:05 p.m. on October 1, 2017, a 64-year-old white male, armed with 24 firearms in total, including automatic rifles[*], action rifles, and revolvers., killed 58 people and wounding 851 others before shooting and killing himself. The perpetrator opened fire from his hotel room, room 32-135 at the Mandalay Bay Hotel and Casino, onto a large crowd of concertgoers at the Route 91 Harvest music festival on the Las Vegas Strip.

---

[*] "Automatic Rifles" or "AR" are interchangeable terms used instead of ArmaLite15.

8. Pittsburgh, Pennsylvania

At approximately 9:05 a.m. on October 27, 2018, a 46-year-old white male, armed with an AR-15[*] and three Glock handguns, killed 11 people and injured 6 in the Tree of Life synagogue located in Pittsburgh, Pennsylvania. The perpetrator surrendered to law enforcement around 11:15 a.m.

9. Tallahassee, Florida

At approximately 5:37 p.m. on November 2, 2018, a 40-year-old white male, armed with a Glock 9mm handgun, shot six people and killed two others in the Tallahassee Hot Yoga studio located in a plaza near other commercial locations in Tallahassee, Florida. The perpetrator was found dead when police arrived.

---

[*] AR = ArmaLite15 is the civilian version of the military's M4 carbine

10. Albuquerque, New Mexico

At approximately 6:15 p.m. on November 12, 2018, a 30-year-old white male blocked an exit with a forklift and began shooting. The perpetrator (a former employee) severely injured three people at the Ben E. Keith Warehouse located in Albuquerque, New Mexico. The perpetrator fled the scene and committed suicide after a long negotiation with the police at around 11:40 p.m. off Interstate 25 near Placitas. It took roughly 5 minutes for law enforcement to arrive.

For more examples, please refer to Appendix B.

Gender

There are several similarities between the perpetrators in this sample group. For example, you may notice the majority of the perpetrators listed above are male. It is widely known, according to the FBI, that the majority of active shooters are male (97%), but a majority is not a totality. (ALERRT, 2016) As you can see, the shooting spree at the San Jose school bus maintenance yard in 2001 and one of the Ben E Keith incidents were perpetrated by a female.

Age

Now notice the range of ages. The average age for active shooters in this list hovered somewhere around the mid 30's. The keywords there is "average," and that concept cannot exist without concepts like "above average," "below average," and "atypical." The 64-year-old Las Vegas shooter was above the average age by roughly thirty years, while the Virginia Tech perpetrator fell below the average by about ten years.

According to the U.S. Secret Service, the below case studies reflect that age truly does not matter:

"YOUNGEST: On January 23, 2018, a 15-year-old sophomore began shooting students randomly in a common area at his high school, killing two and injuring ten. When the attacker ran out of bullets, he abandoned his gun and joined other students who had been hiding. After the students were moved to another room, police identified the attacker and arrested him. The student had planned the attack for about a week, and he did not target any particular students, describing his attack as 'an experiment'." (U.S. Secret Service, 2019)

"OLDEST: On March 7, 2018, a 64-year-old male walked into a local cafe and asked to see the owner, with whom he had a disagreement weeks prior. When the owner appeared, the attacker shot him several times with a rifle, killing him. He then proceeded to shoot cafe patrons, injuring two, and killing one. After the attacker ran out of bullets, he fled to his nearby home and barricaded himself inside. He eventually surrendered to police." (U.S. Secret Service, 2019)

Race

According to the Advanced Law Enforcement Rapid Response Training (ALERRT), 59% of the active shooter incidents from 2000 to 2015 were identified as Caucasian white, while 22% were from Asian, Latino, or other decent, and the rest were African American at 19%. (ALERRT, 2016)

The statistical likelihood obviously does not present any absolute conclusions. Virginia Tech, Washington Navy Yard, Ft. Lauderdale, and San Jose fall outside the norm and once again show us that there will always be outliers in the profiles of active shooters.

Location

As you can also see, the geographical locations for each incident vary quite a bit. Each of them occurred in random spots throughout the United States, from coast to coast and north to south (see Figure 4.3). You've no doubt seen witnesses on the news describing a horrific incident, usually saying something along the lines of, "I never thought this would happen here." This mindset can lull you into a false sense of security. Statistics show that mass shootings are not only on the rise but show no discernible pattern regarding location.

FIGURE 4.3: Active Shooter Geographic – 2016-2017 combined. FBI Map representing 50 active shooter incidents in 21 states. (U.S. Department of Justice, 2018)

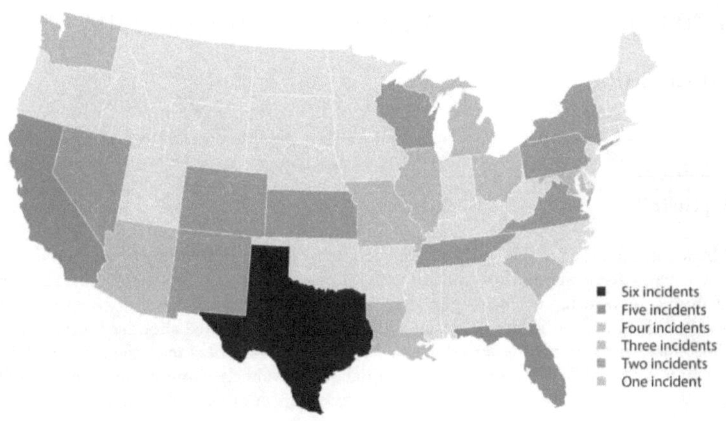

FIGURE 4.4: Active Shooter Geographic – 2018. FBI Map representing 27 active shooter incidents in 16 states. (U.S. Department of Justice, 2018)

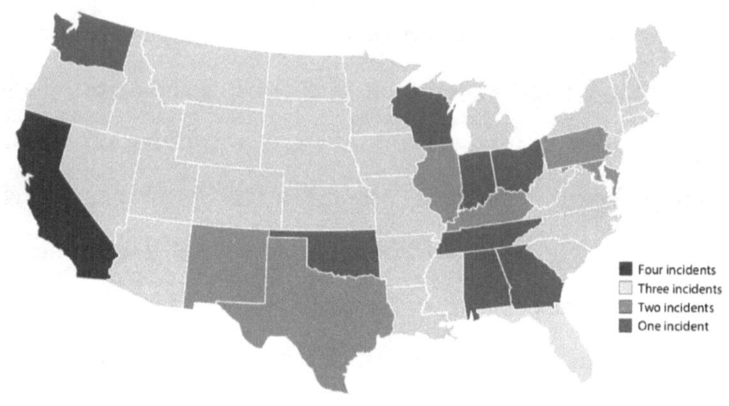

Additional Statistics

An FBI study looked at 277[*] active shooter incidents dating from 2000 to 2018. (U.S. Department of Justice, 2019) The study determined that:

---

[*] See Appendix B.

Note: "Incidents identified in this study do not encompass all gun-related situations; therefore, caution should be taken when using this information without placing it in context. Specifically, shootings that resulted from gang or drug violence—pervasive, long-tracked, criminal acts that could also affect the public— were not included in this study. In addition, other gun-related shootings were not included when those incidents generally appeared not to have put others in peril (e.g., the accidental discharge of a firearm in a school building or a person who chose to publicly commit suicide in a parking lot). The study does not encompass all mass killings or shootings in public places and therefore is limited in its scope." (FBI)

- Only twelve of the incidents involved a female shooter.

- More than one shooter perpetrated only three incidents.

- In at least nine of those incidents, the shooter murdered a family member at home before moving on to a more populated area.

- 52.7% of those 277 incidents came to an end by the shooter's initiative.

  - Committed suicide, fled from the scene, or just ceased shooting entirely before surrendering to law enforcement

- 32.5% of these incidents came to an end when police engaged the shooter in gunfire.

- 13.0% of the incidents were stopped by an unarmed citizen successfully restraining the shooter.

- 43.7% of the incidents occurred in commercial locations.

  - Of these, 30.6% occurred in businesses that are closed to pedestrians.

  - 61.2% occurred in businesses that are open to pedestrians.

  - 8.3% took place at a shopping mall.

- 20.6% occurred in educational locations.

  - Of those, 73.7% in Pre-K through 12th grade.

  - 26.3% occurred in institutions of higher education.

The FBI conducted a study for the calendar year 2016 to 2017, which took a look at 50 active shooter incidents. (U.S. Department of Justice, 2018) The study determined that:

- 50 incidents occurred in 21 states
    - 40% of the incidents met the "mass murder" criteria
    - 100% of the perpetrators were male
    - 6% of the perpetrators wore body armor
    - 26% of the perpetrators committed suicide
    - 22% of the perpetrators were killed by police officers
    - 16% of the perpetrators were stopped by citizens
    - 36% of the perpetrators were apprehended by police
- There were 943 casualties, of which 23.4% were killed, and 76.6% were wounded.
    - 20 law enforcement officers were wounded
    - 13 law enforcement officers were killed during this time period
- 34% of the incidents occurred in commercial locations
    - Of these, 23% occurred in businesses that are closed to pedestrians.
    - 71% occurred in businesses that are open to pedestrians.
    - 6% took place at a shopping mall

- 14% occurred in educational locations
  - Of these, 29% occurred in elementary schools
  - 14% occurred in middle school
  - 57% occurred in high school
- 28% occurred in open spaces
- 6% occurred on government properties
- 4% occurred at residences, houses of worship
- 8% occurred at healthcare facilities
- 2% occurred on a bus

Incident Types

Active shooter incidents typically fall within one of the three following categories:

1. Targeted Attacks
2. Group Attacks
3. Random Attacks

Perpetrators tend to share similar intentions, obviously. They want to inflict terror and cause harm. They are seeking their "15-minutes" of fame. The scope of their intended terror can be very narrow, in that they have a specific person, or people, that they mean to harm. On the other hand, it can be much broader. Their plan may just be to target anyone within their field of vision also known as their field of fire.

By dividing incidents up into one of these three categories, we're able to get even more granular with our analysis. Let's look at some examples of each of these categories:

Targeted Attack:

According to the FBI, there is a direct link in 27% of prior incidents between the perpetrator and the individual(s). Where a targeted attack is, "defined as a person or group of people who were *identifiable before the shooting occurred* and whom the active shooter intended to attack. It was not necessary that the active shooter knew the target by name; intending to attack a person holding a position at or affiliated with a business, educational facility, or in a governmental agency sufficed. The target could be a group, so long as members of that group could have been identified prior to the attack." (Silver, A Study of the Pre-Attack Behaviors of Active Shooters in the United States Between 2000 – 2013, 2018)

For example, on November 5th, 2017 at approximately 11:20 a.m., a 25-year-old white male carried out an attack inside the First Baptist Church in Sutherland Springs, Texas.

The perpetrator was a former U.S. Airman with a string of legal troubles beginning in at least 2012, when he was court-martialed and sentenced to a year in military prison for assaulting his wife and child.

A Facebook page bearing the perpetrators name showed a photo of a Ruger assault-style rifle. Months leading to the killing, the perpetrator had started adding strangers from the Sutherland Springs area as Facebook friends and picking fights with them.

Information gathered after the shooting suggests that the perpetrator's main target was his mother-in-law, Michelle Shields. When the perpetrator first entered the church from an open side door, he fired his Ruger AR-556 semi-automatic rifle toward a corner of the church where Shields had usually sat.

Shields may have been the focus of the perpetrator's violence, but the dozens of casualties show that the perpetrator was willing to kill as many innocent people as possible in order to get to Shields. A total of 26 churchgoers were killed, including Shields' own mother. Twenty more suffered severe injuries.

Unbeknownst to the perpetrator, Shields was not even attending services that day. (Baucum, 2018) A nearby citizen overheard the shots from his home, grabbed his own rifle and shot the perpetrator as he was exiting the church. The perpetrator survived but was badly wounded. He escaped in his truck before taking his own life.

Group Attack

In a group attack, also known as "other", in 36.5% of situations, according to the FBI, "there was a mix of targeted and random victims in the same shooting. The typical circumstance occurred when an active shooter went to a location with targets in mind and shot others who were at the same location, either because they presented some obstacle in the attack or for reasons that could not be identified." (Silver, A Study of the Pre-Attack Behaviors of Active Shooters in the United States Between 2000 – 2013, 2018)

The intent is to kill as many people as possible and the assumption is to kill whoever is in plain sight but move past hard targets. An example would be the Pulse Nightclub Shooting. On June 12, 2016, at 2:00 a.m., a 29-year-old Middle Eastern male entered the Pulse Nightclub in Orlando, Florida armed with a SIG Sauer MCX semi-automatic rifle and a 9mm Glock 17 semi-automatic pistol.

Unlike the Sutherland Springs Church Shooting attack, the Pulse Nightclub attack wasn't focused on killing any one specific person. His intent was to kill as many people as possible. The attack left 49 dead and 53 injured. After a three-hour standoff, Orlando police were able to shoot and kill the perpetrator.

Random Attack

According to the FBI, there is 36.5% of incidents with no link, "in cases where the victims could not reasonably have been identified prior to the shooting, and the active shooter was deemed to have selected the victims at random. Victims of random attacks had: 1) no known connection between the active shooter and the victims, and 2) the victims were not specifically linked to the active shooter's grievance." (Silver, A Study of the Pre-Attack Behaviors of Active Shooters in the United States Between 2000 – 2013, 2018)

The intent varies and the expectation is to kill whoever may be in sight. The Beltway Sniper is an example. Throughout the month of October in 2002, two African American males, ages 41 and 17, randomly targeted their victims with a long-range rifle (Bushmaster XM-15 and .223 Remington/5.56x45mm NATO), throughout Maryland, Virginia and the District of Columbia.

What separates this example from the previous two is the fact that these shooters selected their victims from an opportunistic standpoint. They fired at anyone who happened to be in their crosshairs, one at a time and from a distance. They utilized their blue

1990 Chevrolet Caprice vehicle while one of them laid flat in the trunk of the vehicle shooting sniper-style from a hole near the license plate of the vehicle. The hole allowed the perpetrators to remain hidden and evade authorities during their attacks.

Following a tip, they were arrested while sleeping in a rest stop off Interstate 70 near Myersville, Maryland. According to a CNN interview, "The strongest piece of evidence in this case, the Bushmaster rifle, was found with the perpetrators at the time of their arrest and linked through ballistics testing… the Chevy Caprice in which they were found had a sniper perch and firing port in the trunk." (CNN, 2003) Their three weeklong series of attacks eventually ended with 17 dead and injured 10 (7 people were killed in Washington, Louisiana, Maryland, Georgia, and Alabama before the D.C. attacks).

5

Uncertainty in the Workplace

"There's been a quantum leap technologically in our age, but unless there's another quantum leap in human relations, unless we learn to live in a new way towards one another, there will be a catastrophe."

Albert Einstein

Active Shooter Incidents in the Workplace

With the majority of these incidents occurring in places of business (open to pedestrians or not), employees must become educated and aware of all warning signs or contributing factors that can develop into a mass shooting. These incidents should not just be segmented into the buckets presented below, however. To remain proactive, you must think of your environment as a worker. If you currently work, you are an employee, and therefore a business or organization has put their trust in you.

There are four categories we can place workplace violence into. Some of these forms include:

Four Broad Categories of Workplace Violence

1. Absolute Strangers

These individuals are not affiliated with the workplace in any discernible way. They typically intend to inflict as much damage as possible inside a random location. At times, these shooters may have extremist political or religious views that go against certain businesses. The shooter may also be carrying out a crime, such as a kidnapping or a robbery. Therefore, any shooting done by the perpetrator may be a means to achieve their primary objective.

2. Relatives, Personal Relationships

The shooter may be a relative of an employee or someone who has a close relationship with an employee. Or at least what they perceive as a close relationship. The perpetrator may have a relationship to the employee outside of work that spills over to the work environment.

3. Employees and Supervisors

A dispute between employees boils over to the point that one employee perpetrates a shooting and targets one or more fellow employees, with the possible intent to kill others as collateral damage. Possible examples may include an ex-employee who saw their termination as unfair, a disgruntled subordinate who has decided to take violent action against their superiors, or even a longtime worker who is furious over something like a forced-retirement or a loss of pension.

Bullying is also a major contributing factor in cases of worker-on-worker violence. Verbal or emotional abuse can motivate someone to use violence against their abuser.

4. Customers, clients or patients

The shooter is so dissatisfied by the treatment or service they received from the business that they decide to take revenge by means of violence. Examples of motive may include a dispute over payment or contractual obligations, perceived discrimination, or maybe even something as benign as an expired coupon. These can be returning customers, new customers, prospective clients, third-party vendors, etc. Basically, anyone who has come to the workplace for business purposes in any way.

Those four examples encompass people who may walk into a commercial business, more or less. Consider the following three questions within the context of the previous four examples:

- Would it be out of the ordinary for a customer to walk into your job, be they a new one or a returning one?

- If a relative of yours or a relative of one of your fellow employees walked in, would that set off any mental alarms?

- Would it appear odd to you if an employee or supervisor showed up to work if they weren't scheduled to be in that day?

The answer to all these questions may vary, but more than likely, is no. These examples aren't out of the ordinary. At least not at face value. But if you consider certain factors that often present themselves as common denominators, you may see a common thread, such as a history of violence or substance abuse.

Workplace Violence Risk Factors

The workplace itself can present several risk factors, such as the twelve risk factors depicted in Figure 5.1, which you see below:

FIGURE 5.1: Workplace Violence Risk Factor Matrix

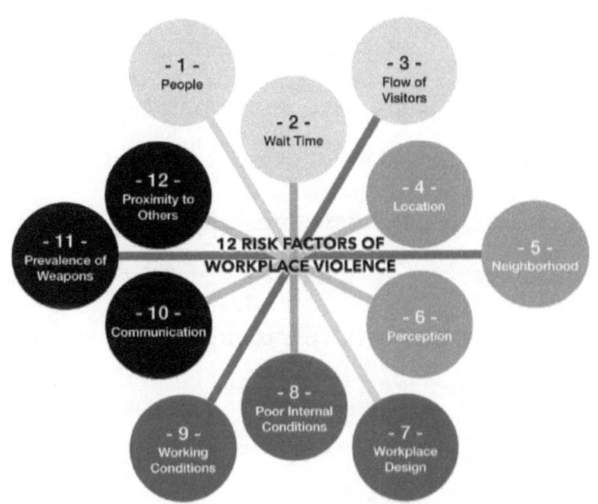

1. People

To conduct business, you need people, guidelines and policies that help manage employee or customer behavior. Organizations are at risk without the appropriate standards in place to mitigate any undesirable behaviors that may pose a liability. Thus, people and their behavior are a risk factor to consider within the workplace violence framework. If a company doesn't have clear expectations written on worker policies and comes up short with their education and training of the employees, especially in regard to rehearsals of active shooter incidents, the risk increases for a hazard to manifest itself into an incident. Consider asking yourself:

- Does my facility have (make available or easily accessible) medication, narcotics, or money?

- Does my facility have individuals (workers, contractors, students, etc.) with a history of violence?

- Does my facility have individuals (workers, contractors, students, etc.) with a history of drug or alcohol abuse?

- Does my facility have individuals that are prone to violence?

2. Wait Time

A customer's experience has a direct link with their satisfaction, which plays a role in overall organizational safety and security. Lack of customer satisfaction may lead to customer impatience. Hence, the second potential risk factor to consider is the wait time. Consider asking yourself:

- Does the facility operate with an inefficient wait time?

- Does the facility typically have an issue with overcrowding?

- Does the facility have cramped waiting rooms?

3. Flow of Visitors

If your workplace has a sort of "free-for-all" policy toward customer service, this may very well become a whole other set of stressors. As an example, if your organization allows people to come and go as they please without little to no oversight, it may increase the potential risk of violence. Risks may develop when customers aren't clear as to where they should line up or whom they should speak to, and employees might be unaware of which customers need to be helped next. Again, these flaws in workplace policy can push both employees and customers to a stressed mindset, which can potentially lead them to make irrational and possibly violent decisions. Thus, the third potential risk factor to consider is the flow of people inside any organization. Consider asking yourself:

- Does the facility operate with the unrestricted movement of people?

- Is the facility monitored with CCTV cameras?

- Does the facility have any safety and security checks and balances?

  o Prevention: Are you dedicating more resources to preventing a threat?

  o Detection: Are you dedicating more resources to detecting hazards?

  o Response: Are you investing in mitigating controls to prevent hazards or threats from repeating?

4. Location/Transportation

Some businesses may require the transportation of assets from one facility to another. The transportation of supplies or people (student/clients/employees) presents the fourth risk factor of workplace violence listed. Consider asking yourself:

- Does my job require transporting goods or services off-site? If so:
    - Does my organization transport supply between facilities or locations?
    - Does my organization transport people between facilities or locations?

5. Neighborhood/Location

Areas with high crime rates can raise the likelihood of an incident, as can a lack of adequate security at the workplace. Although one should not "judge a book by its cover," a business that operates in rough neighborhoods does run a risk in terms of safety and security. Nevertheless, many businesses operate out of low-income neighborhoods with high crime rates. This makes it our fifth risk factor. Consider asking yourself:

- Is my organization located in a neighborhood with a high crime rate?

- Does my organization have inadequate security personnel on site?

6. Perception

Visible signs of crime, or the perception of crime, may encourage more crime and disorder. This is an essential way of thinking of the *"Broken Window Theory"* introduced by social scientists James Q. Wilson and George L. Kelling. Perception is the sixth risk factor. Consider asking yourself:

- Does my organization lend itself to an overall perception that violence is tolerated?

- Does my organization lend itself to an overall perception that victims will not be able to report the incidents to police or leadership?

7. Poor Workplace Design

A building's aesthetics are very important when designing a new building. But apart from its aesthetics, the safety and security of its infrastructure are also considered before breaking ground. Therefore, a balance is necessary when considering the internal physical layout of the building as well. We cannot change the architecture, aesthetics, or potential lack of safety in the physical design of the workplace. But we must be aware of its physical layout strengths and weaknesses in case we need to react during an emergency. Workplace designs that have obstructed views, poor lighting, and crowds/objects in the way of exits are a few examples.

The seventh risk factor to consider is the workplace design. Ask yourself:

- Do you work in an environment with a poor environmental design?

- Do you work in an environment with visibility obstructions, such as beams blocking your vision to the outside?

- Do you work in an environment with anything that provides interference for the potential of escape?

8. Poor Internal Conditions

The physical security of buildings is crucial for the safety and security of businesses. "Physical security" encompasses many layers. Lighting, as an example, is an essential criterion of a building's safety. The clear visibility of pedestrian traffic is vital to keep people safe. Therefore, light, the eighth risk factor, is a strategic advantage of overall safety, both internally and externally. Consider asking yourself:

- Does my facility have poorly lit corridors?

- Does my facility have poorly lit rooms?

- Does my facility have poorly lit parking lots and other areas?

9. Working Conditions

A high rate of turnover or an understaffed workforce make for a stressful work environment and could possibly push some employees over the edge completely. Factors like these can add up to customers dealing with longer wait times or crowded public areas of the business, which can stress out employees and customers/clients/patients alike.

OSHA mandates that "employers have the responsibility to provide a safe and healthful workplace that is free from serious recognized hazards." Employees should not feel stressed while at work due to poor working conditions. This is the ninth risk factor associated with workplace violence. Consider asking yourself:

- Does my organization have periods of understaffed and high work turnover?

- Do the workers feel stressed during peak operational activities?

- Is there a lack of leadership within the work environment?

10. Communication

Communication is a core pillar of leadership. Therefore, the tenth risk factor of workplace violence is the lack of communication within an institution from either a human perspective (leadership) or its core processes (policies and standards). Without clear direction and guidelines from leadership, employees may find it challenging to adapt and manage to an unexpected crisis. Ask yourself:

- Does my organization have policies to manage a crisis within my facility?

- Does my organization conduct training with staff members? If so, how often?

- Does my organizational leadership recognize and manage hostile behaviors efficiently?

11. Prevalence of Weapons

The prevalence of weapons in an environment may be a risk in itself. The public laws about open carry or conceal carry vary throughout the United States. Businesses also have their respective regulations and behaviors about allowing or not allowing patrons to bring firearms into their facilities. Therefore, this is the eleventh risk factor in workplace violence. Consider asking yourself:

- Is there a prevalence of firearms, knives and other weapons inside of the workplace?

12. Proximity to Others

Depending on where you work (location) and the nature of your job (the type of work), you may find yourself alone inside of a facility or with clients. Hence, the final risk factor is the proximity of working next to others.

Potential Impact of Workplace Violence

According to the Occupational Safety and Health Administration (OSHA), American workers have a high reporting rate of workplace violence incidents at work. Over 2 million (2,811,500) American workers reported being victims of workplace violence in 2017. (USDOL BLS, 2018) Workplace violence is "an act or threat of physical violence, harassment, intimidation, or other threatening disruptive behavior that occurs at the work site (or outside of work that migrates to work). It ranges from threats and verbal abuse to physical assaults and even homicide. It can affect and involve employees, clients, customers and visitors." (USDOL, n.d.)

As a business owner or leader within the organization, ignoring a workplace violence issue can be costly and a risk. Its impact on the overall business can be felt throughout the entire organization. These business impacts manifest as either direct costs or indirect costs.

Several of the direct costs associated with workplace violence claims are: 1) the cost associated with a potential need for critical incident care due to post-traumatic stress disorder, 2) the cost associated with a potential temporary closure, 3) the cost associated with a potential loss of revenue, 4) the cost associated with a potential healthcare premium increase, 5) the cost associated with a potential rise in workers' comp premiums, 6) the cost associated with a potential cost of litigation, and 7) the cost associated with a potential expenses associated employee turnover. (Walker, 2019)

Although the direct costs are potentially manageable by many organizations with significant financial resources, the indirect costs are much harder to manage and potentially irreversible. Workplace violence draws unwanted negative publicity, undesired loss of productivity (business interruption), potential employee turnover, probable drop in morale and job satisfaction, fearful atmosphere, difficult employee retention, and potentially long-lasting psychological trauma.

Business leaders have a fiduciary duty to keep people and their property free of risks. People should be safe and without any threat of violence, no matter where they may live. Unfortunately, violence at work has transcended beyond traditional environments and impacted many people throughout the globe. Consider this quote from the World Health Organization:

"Workplace violence — be it physical or psychological — has become a global problem crossing borders, work settings, and occupational groups. For long a forgotten issue, violence at work has dramatically gained momentum in recent years and is now a priority concern in both industrialized and developing countries." (World Health Organization, 2002)

Stages of Workplace Violence

Workplace violence can be a spontaneous event, or it can present itself in multiple stages of escalation. They require immediate attention to mitigate against impulsive actions that are detrimental to both the person and the organization. As demonstrated in *Violence Goes to College: The Authoritative Guide to Prevention, Intervention, and Response*, "humans, are strongly verbal-oriented and tend to pay attention to what people say. Too often, however, we ignore the discrepancy between what is said and how it is said and go only with the literal spoken word. When someone's verbal and nonverbal signals are incongruent, the nonverbal communication is almost always more reflective of the true emotional state." (Christopher Bollinger, 2018)

For example, physical assault has the potential to escalate all the way to deadly assault. "Physically destructive or abusive conduct could reflect a deteriorated internal state or poor impulse control," which is a warning sign of violence in itself. (Ibid) Some examples of physical assault include beatings, stabbings, sexual assault, or rape. The top left-hand box of Figure 5.2 displays the levels of escalation for physical assault.

A person's verbal and body language which are manipulative, intimidating, and control the behavior of others are strong indicators of future behavior. These behaviors "suggest the individual has minimal coping and/or interpersonal skills." Verbal abuse can also escalate from a minimal level all the way to verbal assault. The bottom left hand box of Figure 5.2 displays these levels of escalation. Examples of verbal abuse can include blaming others, obscene phone calls, teasing, and name calling.

Threatening behavior is the most serious as it involves verbal or non-verbal threats which may lead to a physical altercation or verbal abuse. The top right-hand box of Figure 5.2 displays examples such as blaming others with intense language intimidation.

FIGURE 5.2: Workplace Violence Escalation

Physical Assault	**Threatening Behavior**

• **Complaint** > Fully Cooperative
• **Passive Resistant** > Subtle Defiance
• **Active Resistant** > Slamming Doors, Turning over desks
• **Assault** > Physical Fights, attempt to hurt others
• Deadly Assault
	• Most Serious
	• Intimidating others with language
	  • Verbal
	    • Intense, blaming others, using the word "you" in an accusatory tone
	• Nonverbal threats

Verbal Abuse	**Forms of Behavior**
• **Complaint** > Normal interaction • **Negative** > Frequently complains & responds negatively to helpful advice • **Abusive** > General nastiness • **Derogatory** > Vulgar, racist, sexist • **Verbal Assaulting/Threatening**: Greatest Risk (bizarre & destructive)	• Harassment • Bullying • Domestic violence • Stalking • Emotional abuse • Intimidation

The bottom right hand box of Figure 5.2 displays forms of hostile behavior typically found in the workplace. They are: harassment, bullying, domestic violence, stalking, emotional abuse, cyberbullying and intimidation.

There are many examples of organizations across various industries impacted by workplace violence. No industry is immune. Recent examples of workplace violence will help you see how this epidemic has affected several organizations and people via harassment, sexual assault, termination, or mass shooting. Some were spontaneous while some slowly escalated.

Harassment:

- The Unified Government of Wyandotte County and Kansas City, Kansas is managing the aftermath of a jury's conviction against a longtime supervisor who was charged with misdemeanor battery against a female employee. (The Kansas City Star Editorial Board, 2019)

- The Weinstein Company has lost its business due to the felony charges against former Hollywood producer Harvey Weinstein. Weinstein has faced serious charges related to sexual assault and harassment. (Paul, 2019)

Sexual Assault:

- The University of Arizona is also facing hostile workplace investigation following reports of an alleged sexual assault involving football players and a "culture of sexual harassment in the football program." (Schmidt, 2019)

- An employee at the Medical University of South Carolina was sexually assaulted by a patient after the patient was moved to a secluded room. (Wildeman, 2019)

Termination:

- Following the termination of an employee from Burris Logistics, an ex-employee was arrested "after he allegedly assaulted his supervisor" and then "threatened to kill everyone in the building." (Hamilton, 2019)

- A United Airline flight attendant was arrested for public intoxication while working on the August 2, 2019, flight traveling from Chicago to Indiana. The flight attendant on board was "slurring her speech" and was unable to walk straight during the flight. (Deerwester, 2019)

Mass Shooting:

- The above Burris Logistics incident is an example of a workplace violence event that could have been catastrophic had it not been reported to the police. Unfortunately, Walmart, Ned Peppers Bar, and the Marriot were impacted by mass shooting incidents during July and August of 2019.

- On July 30, 2019, two Walmart employees were shot by a former employee. Several days before the shooting, the perpetrator (a former Walmart employee) brandished a knife to co-workers, which led to his suspension. (Natalie Neysa Alund, 2019)

- On August 3, 2019, a perpetrator killed 22 people and wounded 24 others at a Walmart store located in El Paso, Texas. The FBI is investigating the incident as a possible hate crime and domestic terrorism. (Bates, 2019)

- In less than 24 hours, the city of Dayton, Ohio also experienced an active shooter in a Ned Peppers Bar located in Dayton, Ohio's bar district. The incident left ten people dead and 27 others injured. (Zennie, 2019)

- On August 21, 2019, the Police Department of Long Beach, CA arrested a disgruntled employee who threatened to commit mass murder at his workplace. The perpetrator had "clear plans, intent and the means to carry out an act of violence that may have resulted in a mass casualty incident." (Wigglesworth, 2019)

6

The Importance of Observation

"Paying attention and awareness are universal capacities of human beings."

Jon Kabat-Zinn

Motivation is an important aspect of productivity and success. Can one achieve a goal if they're completely lacking the motivation to do so? Most likely not.

Can a lawyer successfully cross interrogate a witness if he or she is not motivated to win the case? Can a star athlete flawlessly break records if they don't give everything they have? Can an employee become a CEO if they do not reflect the skills and motivation to lead? No, no, and no.

I believe motivation is a key factor to a lot of the things we do from the moment we start the day. We use it daily to do something, *anything*, that will enable us to accomplish our personal goals and surpass our career aspirations. It serves as our driving force and keeps one foot in front of the other.

But motivation can be a force for evil just as much as it can be a force for good. So, what motivates an active shooter to act on their plan?

According to the FBI's research, there are fifteen "stressors" that provide insight to possible motivations for a person to commit a crime. Stressors are invisible and hard to detect unless you are at least somewhat familiar with the person who may be exhibiting them. They are, "physical, psychological, or social forces that place real or perceived demands/pressures on an individual and which may cause psychological and/or physical distress. Stress is considered to be a well-established correlate of criminal behavior." (Felson, 2012) The analyzed stressors can range from financial pressures, to physical health concerns, to interpersonal conflicts with family, friends, and colleagues, just to name a few.

As mentioned earlier, the totality of circumstances should be applied here. Just because someone is going through financial pressures or has interpersonal conflicts with a family member does not mean they are a threat or will commit a crime. In fact, the FBI selected data from previous active shooter incidents between 2000-2013 that reflected "adverse impact on that individual, and which were sufficiently significant to have been memorialized, shared, or otherwise noted in some way (e.g., in the active shooter's own writings, in conversation with family or friends, work files, court records)." (Silver, A Study of the Pre-Attack Behaviors of Active Shooters in the United States Between 2000 – 2013, 2018)

FIGURE 6.1: 15 Possible Stressors in Active Shooter Perpetrators (Silver, A Study of the Pre-Attack Behaviors of Active Shooters in the United States Between 2000 – 2013, 2018)

Invisible: 15 memorialized stressors in prior incidents

"Physical, psychological, or social forces that place real or perceived demands/pressures on an individual and which may cause psychological and/or physical distress. Stress is considered to be a well-established correlate of criminal behavior."

- 62% - Mental health problems	- 49% - Financial strain	- 29% - Conflict with friends/peers	Other: Misanthropy
- 27% - Marital problems	- 35% - Job-related problems	- 22% - School-related problems	Other: Perceived Injustice
- 22% - Abuse of illicit drugs or alcohol	- 21% - Physical injury	- 18% - Conflict with parents	Other: Revenge
- 13% - Sexual stress/frustration	- 11% - Criminal legal problems	- 16% - Conflict with other family members	Other: Ideological Extremism
- 6% - Death of friend/relative	- 10% - Civil legal problem	- 22% - Other	Other: Notoriety

Figure 6.1 itemizes each pre-attack stressor with their respective percentage in which it may have influenced the perpetrator before the incident occurred. For example, financial strain was a stressor in 49% of the perpetrators, job-related problems were a factor in 35% of the cases, followed by conflict with people, marital problems, or civil legal problems, amongst others. In

Appendix A, I provide a further explanation with the definition for each stressor.

FIGURE 6.2: 21 Potential Concerning Behaviors in Active Shooter Perpetrators (Silver, A Study of the Pre-Attack Behaviors of Active Shooters in the United States Between 2000 – 2013, 2018)

Observable: 21 concerning behaviors in prior incidents

Concerning behaviors are observable behaviors exhibited by the active shooter.		
- 62% - Mental health	**- 33% -** Anger	**- 11% -** Impulsivity
- 57% - Interpersonal interactions	**- 33% -** Physical Aggression	**- 10% -** Alcohol Abuse
- 56% - Leakage	**- 21% -** Risk-taking	**- 10% -** Physical Health
- 54% - Quality of thinking or communication	**- 21% -** Firearm behavior	**- 6% -** Sexual Behavior
- 46% - Work performance	**- 19% -** Violent media usage	**- 5% -** Quality of Sleep
- 42% - School performance	**- 13% -** Weight/eating	**- 3% -** Hygiene/appearance
- 35% - Threats/confrontations	**- 13% -** Drug Abuse	**- 8% -** Other

On the other hand, there were 21 "concerning behaviors" identified by the FBI to help you remain aware and proactive before danger might strike. (Silver, A Study of the Pre-Attack Behaviors of Active Shooters in the United States Between 2000 – 2013, 2018) The behaviors listed on Figure 6.2 were observable characteristics exhibited by the active shooter. Furthermore, other people knew and detected these behaviors in the individuals before they converted to a terrorist active shooter. Individuals that knew the person beforehand, felt a "more than minimal" degree of unease about their well-being and the safety of those around the individual. (Ibid) This is very important considering the previous list of 15 stressors were factors that active shooters were personally struggling with but hard to detect. They acted based on a combination of those stressors and these concerning behaviors. It's just another example of the totality of circumstances that have been mentioned previously.

The characteristics range from interpersonal interactions, leakage, quality of thinking or communication, work performance and anger, amongst other behaviors. In Appendix A, I also provide a further explanation with the definition to each concerning behavior.

Possible Motives

Active shooters are unique individuals, just like the rest of us. Yes, they all decided to inflict violence upon innocent people, but the combination of factors that drove them to that point are where their differences lie. But by starting with each shooter's specific motive and following the stem, we find that many active shooter incidents seem to share the very same root.

Obviously, there is absolutely no way to predict with total certainty that someone will become an active shooter, but by observing the aforementioned 16 stressors, 21 concerning warning signs and paying particular attention to people we know or observing certain behaviors in other people, we begin to see the parallels and analyze patterns within the totality of circumstances.

Here are several case studies that provide examples of previous perpetrator's possible motives and warning signs:

Case Study #1

Perpetrator #1 Exhibited:

- Increased isolation, depression, detachment, withdrawn behaviors
- Paranoid or delusional statements
- Empathy toward violent offenders
- Uncontrollable anger, outbursts of rage
- History of violence or psychiatric treatment
- Suicidal statements

The 2013 Washington Navy Yard Shooting perpetrated by a 34-year-old African American male is an example of what can happen when poor mental health motivates an individual to commit mass murder. The behaviors and personality traits observed by those who knew the perpetrator were remarkably similar to other active shooters who faced mental health challenges.

One month prior to the Washington Navy Yard shooting, the perpetrator had filed a police report in Rhode Island, in which he said he was facing harassment and hearing voices in his head. (Andersen, 2013) He also claimed that "ELF," or "extremely low frequency electromagnetic waves," were trying to gain influence and control over him. (Ian Simpson, 2013) Upon investigation into his personal computing devices, authorities found the following message, written by the Washington Navy Yard perpetrator:

> *"Ultra-low frequency attack is what I've been subject to for the last 3 months. And to be perfectly honest, that is what has driven me to this."*

The Washington Navy Yard perpetrator's belief that outside forces were attempting to overpower his mental faculties is a classic example of delusion and paranoia that mentally ill shooters typically exhibit. Further examples of this were found written on the murder weapon itself. The perpetrator's Remington 12-gauge shotgun had the following phrases scratched into the metal:

> *"Better off this way!"*
> *"My ELF weapon!"*
> *"Not what yall say!"*
> *"End to this torment!"*

Case Study #2

As documented by the FBI's study of active shooters between 2000 and 2013, "a grievance is defined as the cause of the active shooter's distress or resentment; a perception — not necessarily based in reality — of having been wronged or treated unfairly or inappropriately." They elaborate by stating that a grievance is, "more than a typical feeling of resentment or passing anger, it often results in a grossly distorted preoccupation with a sense of injustice, like an injury that fails to heal. These thoughts can saturate a person's thinking and foster a pervasive sense of imbalance between self-image. Humiliation begins to boil, eventually to a point that the subject cannot bear. At this point, they may devise a plan to 'right the wrong' in the hopes of restoring what they perceive as a balance." (Silver, A Study of the Pre-Attack Behaviors of Active Shooters in the United States Between 2000 – 2013, 2018)

A shooter who was driven to kill others based on some sort of unfair treatment, whether real or imagined, will often exhibit the following behaviors:

- Outrage and blame toward others for a perceived injustice
- Threats of violence, both verbal and non-verbal
- Stalking

- Hostility toward those who have slighted them
- Inability to manage stress from relationships, bullying, emotional trauma, etc.

The Sutherland Springs, Texas Church Shooting perpetrated by a 25-year-old white male serves as an example of this motivating factor. The Texas Church Shooting perpetrator's attack came from his belief that the actions of others left him with no choice.

The Texas Church Shooting perpetrator felt he had a number of issues with his mother-in-law, most likely due to the fact that she was unhappy with her daughter being married to someone with a criminal record and a history of violence. He had spent a year in a military prison for assaulting his first wife and their child. He had also been charged with cruelty toward animals in a 2014 incident. (Eli Rosenberg, 2017)

While the mother-in-law was the shooter's main target, the rest of the church's attendees were to be collateral damage. He stormed in and first fired toward a row of pews where his mother-in-law usually sat. (She was not in attendance that day, unbeknownst to him.) (Ibid)

After the shooting, the mother-in-law, Michelle Shields, provided a number of examples that illustrated the Texas Church Shooting perpetrator's hatred towards her, including text messages in which he explicitly threatened violence toward Ms. Shields if she were to come to the hospital to witness the birth of her own granddaughter. (Foster-Frau, 2018) One of the text messages read, "I will personally make it my mission to destroy your entire life. I suggest you don't test my resolve." (Ibid)

While the Texas Church Shooting perpetrator had a well-documented history of violent behavior and poor choices, he had shifted the blame away from himself and onto others, namely Shields. This is a classic behavior pattern among many active shooters.

Case Study #3

Acts of extreme violence can sometimes be the byproduct of extreme hatred, also known as "misanthropy." Possible behavioral indicators can include:

- Verbal statements of hatred toward a particular person or group
- Hostility toward those who are different
- Participation in and/or sympathy for groups that espouse hate and violence
- Xenophobic comments or threats

The Emanuel African Methodist Episcopal Church in downtown Charleston, South Carolina incident of June 17, 2015 serves as a perfect example of this motivation.

The South Carolina church perpetrator's internet/social media presence prior to the shooting displayed numerous signs of racial hatred. (Robles, 2015) Images showed the perpetrator wearing patches on his jacket that are often associated with white supremacy. These patches included the Rhodesian flag, the Confederate flag, and the flag of South Africa. (Sari Horwitz, 2015)

The manifesto published by the perpetrator, as well as answers he gave during police questioning, indicated that the perpetrator's goal was to incite a race war between blacks and whites. (Hersher, 2016) Some of the elements contained in the manifesto discussed his views on the racial awakening inspired by the Trayvon Martin incident; he claimed to have been educated by organized white supremacists following his research into the Martin case; he also claimed to have been inspired by apartheid in South Africa and the American Confederacy; the perpetrator also wrote about the role of slavery in the history of the U.S. and how it influenced him and his views on races. (Yglesias, 2015)

In the manifesto itself the perpetrator writes: "I have no choice. I am not in the position to, alone, go into the ghetto and fight. I chose Charleston because it is most historic city in my state, and at one time had the highest ratio of blacks to Whites in the country. We have no skinheads, no real KKK, no one doing anything but talking on the internet. Well someone has to have the bravery to take it to the real world, and I guess that has to be me." (The Guardian, n.d.) and (Buncombe, 2015)

Case Study #4

Ideological extremism is similar to misanthropy but is typically driven by extreme views of a religious or political nature. Indicators may include:

- Extreme social, religious or political views in conjunction with threats
- Angry and violent rhetoric
- Hatred toward those who do not share the same beliefs or values

The Fort Hood, Texas shooting of November 5, 2009, serves as a noteworthy example. The shooter's six years as an intern at the Walter Reed National Military Medical Center raised some red flags for those who worked closely with him. His job performance would often be poor, and the comments he made were often received by colleagues and superiors as inappropriate and troubling. (NPR News, 2009) For example, "in late 2008, nearly a year before his attack, the perpetrator captured the attention of the FBI when he began emailing Anwar al-Aulaqi, an American, English-speaking radical cleric in Yemen; al-Aulaqi was under FBI investigation and widely viewed as one of the most influential "virtual spiritual sanctioners" of terrorism in the world." (Zegart, 2015)

The perpetrator showed signs of social isolation and was often overcome with job-related stress. (Ibid) Stories of warfare experiences that were shared with him by soldiers (he was a psychiatrist in the Army) brought on obvious signs of frustration and disillusionment toward serving in the armed forces.

One month prior to the shooting, the perpetrator was scheduled to be deployed to Afghanistan. He gave away many of his belongings to his neighbor, a typical behavior among those who are planning an act that could result in their death or possibly long-term incarceration. (Brick, 2009) He also made comments to fellow military members that were perceived as anti-American during this time. (The Associated Press, 2009)

Additional Considerations

In addition to these potential motives and warning signs, there are a number of what can be referred to as "aggravated factors." These are circumstances that can reinforce the shooter's troubled mindset and blur the line between rational and irrational decision making. Examples include:

- Increase of Substance abuse
- Increase in violence or violent threats
- Obsession with weapons, usually manifesting itself as stockpiling or arming themselves at all times
- Making direct statements about carrying out a violent attack

Communication is Critical

At some point in the time leading up to these attacks, each of the shooters displayed a combination of these factors (stressors or concerning behaviors) in one way or another. It's easy to ignore these signs or write them off as the typical behavior of a genuinely odd person but recognizing these behaviors and communicating them to others is the first step toward prevention. The second step is highly dependent on the entities that receive the warning. I would suggest adding a third step - follow-up and ensure some kind of action was actually taken.

But what additional indicators can we look out for? Sometimes, they are right in plain sight. There is no doubt there is a lot to consider when you are trying to remain aware of stressors, precursor warning signs, or concerning behaviors. But it is important to know how people may potentially communicate to you by analyzing the known methods of communication available in order to remain proactive and mitigate the potential of danger. The FBI breaks the concerning communication into two categories, which are "threats/confrontations" and "leakage."

According to the FBI, perpetrators have had a history of making comments that state their intent for violence, often towards their respective target directly. This communication may start directly from the perpetrator. 55% of perpetrators have done so in-person through confrontations intended to intimidate. These comments may be made via online mediums or in person (nonverbal or verbal). The chosen means of communication have been through text messages, emails, telephone, or social media. (Silver, A Study of the Pre-Attack Behaviors of Active Shooters in the United States Between 2000 – 2013, 2018)

Secondly, perpetrators have had a history of leaking their intent to a third party (clues with intent of violent act). 56% of perpetrators have leaked their feelings, thoughts, fantasies, attitudes, or intentions through verbal, written, or online statements. (Ibid)

The third category includes the 30% of the perpetrators which have deliberately communicated their intentions through a "legacy token." These are communications that may place the perpetrator on the path to claim the credit for their act. This has been done via manifestos, videos, social media posts that are staged for discovery post-incident. (Ibid)

Communication is key when someone notices a cluster of the previously discussed warning signs. 89% of the previously analyzed incidents by the FBI noted four formats in which perpetrators demonstrated concerning behaviors. (Silver, A Study of the Pre-Attack Behaviors of Active Shooters in the United States Between 2000 – 2013, 2018)

1. The perpetrator verbalized 95% of the communication
2. 86% of the physical actions were observed in the perpetrator
3. 27% of the perpetrators communicated via writing
4. 16% of the perpetrators displayed their behavior online

If you realize a cluster of warning signs within the totality of circumstances, you must say something. If you take no action, it is a missed opportunity to save lives.

The people most likely to notice concerning behaviors are family members, friends, coworkers, and/or classmates. According to the FBI, 54% of people that noticed concerning behaviors in previous perpetrators did not communicate any concerning behaviors because of loyalty, disbelief, or fear of consequences. (Ibid)

There were a handful of people that decided to communicate their concerning observations. In 83% of the incidents, the common method of communication to help mitigate the risk was communicating directly with the perpetrator. (Ibid) In 51% of the incidents, the perpetrators decided to report the threat to non-law enforcement. (Ibid) In 49% of the incidents, it was discussed with friends and family, while 41% chose to report the threats directly to law enforcement. (Ibid)

Concerning Communication

Threat/confrontations, as defined by the FBI, are "direct communications to a target of intent to harm and may be delivered in person (to intimidate or cause safety concerns) or by other means (e.g., text, email, telephone)." (Ibid)

Leakage, on the other hand, refers to "when a person intentionally or unintentionally reveals clues to a third-party about feelings, thoughts, fantasies, attitudes, indirect thoughts of harm, legacy tokens (manifestos/ online posts discovered minutes after the incident) or intentions that may signal the intent to commit a violent act (innuendo about a desire to commit a violent attack, or boasts about the ability to harm others)." (Ibid) A leakage can be found on many mediums of communication from traditional forms of writings (journals) or on cloud-based communication portals. (tweets, blogs, etc.)

If you happen to find yourself in a situation where someone may signal the intent to commit a violent act, consider listening to what they are saying and how they are saying it. Be sure to document it as well. You may be hesitant do so, but you must always consider "the totality of circumstances." Motives, warning signs (stressors or concerning behaviors) and aggravated factors come in all different forms, and the combination of the behaviors which stem from these factors always have the potential to add up to an active shooter incident. Therefore, if you see these behaviors or hear someone blatantly making a threat, whether directly or indirectly, you *must* report them immediately.

Here is an example that may illustrate leakage and the importance of observing odd behaviors and acting appropriately, while also not jumping to conclusions.

On December 12, 2018, my client notified me of a threat posted on Instagram. My client, Mr. Buller, forwarded a picture from what appeared to be taken from his staff's telephone. I realized the characteristics of the account were a bit off. The account name read "ill damage your school" and its username read "schoolhouse_killer." Furthermore, the account had zero posts, two followers, and a message that read "VP Students and everyone who tends there will die." I froze when I read the message and saw the picture. It took me several minutes to gather my thoughts and create an action plan.

Within five minutes, I responded to my client and asked, "Have authorities been notified? And have threats like these happened before? If so, how were they handled?" It was great to hear that law enforcement was in fact, contacted and the police were going to be at the school in the morning. With this in mind, I still wanted to do more and ensure that I took the appropriate steps to notify anyone else that needed to be notified. The single thought that went through my mind was "if something happens and I did nothing, I will feel horrible and responsible."

I had my team contact Facebook and Instagram about this account to flag it immediately. While my team handled that communication, I reached out directly to the FBI. I felt it was my fiduciary duty as a business owner to help mitigate the threat with their assistance. But I also felt morally responsible for notifying the FBI as a private citizen. After the phone call, I felt a bit of relief because all possible angles were managed within the best of our abilities — the social media angle, local, state, and federal law enforcement. (KLFY, 2018)

Here is another example of communicating a threat. On February 15, 2018, Angela McDevitt became a hero in the state of Vermont. (Nina Keck, 2019) McDevitt recognized a warning sign that shocked her. Before the February 14th Marjory Stoneman Douglas High School, Parkland incident she and Jack Sawyer were chatting online. On February 11th, Sawyer mentioned to McDevitt, "Just a few days ago, I was still plotting on shooting up my old high school." At first, she was in disbelief. She eventually realized the severity of the statement, and her sense of awareness was heightened. She then took proactive steps. After hearing of the Parkland incident, McDevitt messaged Sawyer about it. Sawyers response was as follows:

Text messages allegedly sent by Jack Sawyer to Angela McDevitt. (CBS News, 2018)

"That's fantastic… 100% support it."

McDevitt was shocked, and replied, "You can't say that… people are dead." That was the moment she decided to communicate the information to local authorities. She did so the following morning, on February 15, 2018. By noon of that day, Sawyer was arrested. He was not able to follow through with his plot.

Here is a third example: On August 10, 2019, a 26-year-old Winter Park, Florida native was arrested for making direct online threats on Facebook. The individual wrote, "3 more days of probation left then I get my AR-15 back. Don't go to Walmart next week." (WFTS Digital Staff , 2019) This individual, according to investigators, had a history of posting online threats, so law enforcement took swift action in order to mitigate any risk following the El Paso, Texas and Dayton, Ohio shootings that occurred the week prior.

Before we move on, let's look at one more example: On August 8, 2019, "a 20-year-old Springfield, Missouri native was arrested for wearing body armor and carrying a loaded rifle — and more than 100 rounds of ammunition — at a Walmart store." (Bill Chappel, 2019) This incident was right after the El Paso and Dayton incidents and obviously caused major havoc among the citizens of Springfield. Although Missouri is an open carry state, the manner in which this 20-year old displayed his weapon inside of Walmart may have broken the law. His confrontational attitude goes against the state of Missouri laws since they "prohibit gun owners from displaying their weapons in a threatening way. Missouri protects the right of people to open carry a firearm, but that does not allow an individual to act in a reckless and criminal manner endangering other citizens." (Bill Chappel, 2019)

Part Two:

Perspectives on Options

"We hope all danger may be overcome; but to conclude that no danger may ever arise would itself be extremely dangerous."

Abraham Lincoln

7

Key Strategies

*"Strategy without tactics is the slowest route to victory.
Tactics without strategy is the noise before defeat."*

Sun Tzu

We've gone over examples of incidents and the warning signs that preceded them, but now it's time for us to turn our focus to the threats themselves.

There may come a time in your life in which you find yourself in a life-or-death crisis, not unlike the ones we've previously mentioned. These situations will put you to the ultimate test. Will you let the fear and shock overcome you, or will you dig deep and allow that fear to work in your favor so that it can boost your resolve, resiliency, determination, and grit?

The truth is, you won't know until it happens. But by implementing risk management techniques, you can help increase the odds of survival for both yourself and those around you. Survival is paramount. Especially when confronted with or caught in the middle of an unexpected life or death situation involving an active shooter who intends to inflict major carnage.

During the moment, you may find yourself among the many people that may have to make their own individual choices for survival, or you may decide to help others. Either way, having a mental plan to survive should be your strategic priority before you enter any facility.

In a proactive state, you are anticipating the future and you are reacting to the environment accordingly. As a strategy and as a tactic, innovation also plays a fundamental role in staying ahead of unexpected situations. For example, reflect back to a time in your life when you had to be creative and had to innovate to get out of a non-life-threatening situation. You may have had to think on your toes and quickly pivot to survive that particular moment.

In the Marine Corps, adapting and overcoming through innovation is fundamentally engrained in us so that we have the ability to survive though unexpected situations and tough environments. Not reacting or reacting too late may put you at a great disadvantage. Doing nothing is never a strategy one should follow.

As humans, we have biases, as much as we'd hate to admit it. They can be innate or they could have been learned over time, but they always cause us to lean in favor or against a particular thing –

such as the elements around us that may indicate a threat. Teach yourself to be honest about your reality, and don't close your mind off to any possible scenarios, no matter how unpleasant they might seem. Consistently claiming "that won't happen in this town/business/school/place of worship" is dangerous. We need to switch off that mindset of denial and be prepared at all times.

It is common for people confronted with a threat to first deny the possible danger rather than respond. After all, it's only human nature to first try to comprehend what is going on around us before taking any action. After all, wouldn't you prefer the feeling of safety over the feeling of dread? Of course, you would. But denying the danger, even in those first few seconds may prolong your chances of surviving an incident. By being in denial, your number of options decreases with each passing second.

In 2005, the National Institute of Standards and Technology conducted a study into the collapse of the World Trade Center towers on 9/11. Their study showed that people who were closer to the affected floors waited longer to start evacuating than those on the unaffected floors. (Averill, 2005)

The report found that "while a significant event, not all occupants felt their lives were in danger initially. Of the survivors in World Trade Center 1 (WTC 1), 41% felt their life was at risk, and 48% felt others' lives were at risk, at first awareness. Only 4% of the survivors reported being injured by the attack initially, while only 6% reported others being injured." (Ibid)

People often deny and deny until they can validate something is amiss. Once they receive confirmation, they feel comfortable to act by implementing a strategy and tactic. During the World Trade Center attack, 70% of survivors that participated in interviews reported they spoke to others before evacuating, 46% gathered personal items, and 30% helped others. (Ibid)

A survivor who was around the 90th floor of one of the towers later told the media, "I heard a sound that sounded like a giant aluminum can being crushed and I felt the building tilt. I tried calling my company's home office but the line for long distance calls was not in service. I called home to test the phones and to let my family know that I was okay. I checked to see if our server was still up. I saw a man bleeding. I got a first aid kit and succeeded in halting the man's bleeding. We saw debris and smoke and decided it was time to get out. I got my briefcase, a fire extinguisher, and four diet sodas, exited into the hallway and went towards stairwell C." (Ibid)

Similarly, during the April 16, 2007 Virginia Tech shooting, individuals on campus responded to the shooting with varying degrees of urgency. Many of them had a delayed response or exhibited the classic signs of denial. The University sent out a notification, but many were not aware or just flat out chose to ignore it. One student said, "she walked toward her class, preoccupied with an upcoming exam and listening to music on her iPod. On the way, she said, she heard some loud cracks, and only later concluded they had been gunshots from the second round of shootings." (O'connor, 2007) It was also documented that "many students were walking around the campus with little if any sense of alarm" (Ibid) and while the sound of gunfire broke out, they were convinced that they were hearing firecrackers go off.

What is the best strategy to ensure people are responsive during these initial and critical moments? It depends. But I would say it is training and learning how to manage stress under extreme circumstances. During the professional development courses that I teach, I ask my clients how often their emergency response trainings are conducted and how receptive their personnel are toward the training. Are emergency drills conducted regularly? If so, is someone documenting what occurred with the lessons learned? Take a moment to answer those questions for yourself. But most importantly, ask yourself if you see training exercises as just another work duty that needs to be marked off the occasional checklist, or if you see them as crucial facets of safety and security. Because if you look at it as just another chore, then chances are you're not taking it seriously enough.

There are inherit benefits for training personnel on safety and security matters. (See Figure 7.1 for more benefits on safety and security professional development.) For starters, any location is at risk of an active shooter threat, as we discussed earlier. So, training your personnel on safety and security will introduce the element of risk and provide a "taste" of how to manage uncertainty. It will also show that you put their safety first.

To help against potential lawsuits and compensation claims, human resource departments should consider conducting regular safety and security training sessions. Neglecting such professional development may add up to a high cost down the road, one that would be much higher than it would be to invest in empowering your staff with the proper skillset to stay injury free and safe. Leaders should train their personnel frequently and in a low stress environment, as these are the only times in which you can afford to fail. Your team will practice together and learn how to work cohesively.

Your brand image will also improve through the process. Otherwise, it all could add up to an indirect cost that you cannot afford. It is difficult to take corrective action and right the wrong through a public relation strategy.

Personnel will learn from these mistakes and develop the respective muscle memory needed to react accordingly. The more you train, the easier it will be to bypass denial in order to act immediately. Trained personnel will always react with a wider perspective on what is expected compared to those personnel that may not have any training.

FIGURE 7.1: Benefits of Safety and Security Professional Development

Benefits of Safety and Security Professional Development	
Consider balancing business operations with safety and security.	
1	Introduce the element of risk and emergency response procedures into your business.
2	Shows you truly care for their safety and it will increase staff productivity. The staff will learn how to react to unexpected environmental situational changes.
3	Comply with federal and state laws.
4	Mitigate against the potential of a lawsuit or compensation claims.
5	Hedge against indirect costs and boost your brand image.
6	Build team cohesiveness and learn from mistakes in a low stress environment.
7	Build muscle memory through repetition.
8	Build a mental model on how to respond and pivot dependent on the situation.

To further illustrate this point, let's consider a few more examples of how several World Trade Center survivors reacted when realizing their lives were in danger:

An occupant from a floor in the 60s in WTC 1 told the media "It felt like the building was going to fall over. I grabbed my bag to leave the office floor. I was not waiting for anyone to tell me what to do." Another occupant from a floor in the 20s of the WTC 1 stated, "I waited for the building to stop shifting. I began to run straight out the nearest exit out of my office towards Stairway B. It was the nearest exit from my office and co-workers were just saying let's go this way." (Averill, 2005)

What to Do?

Adversarial and human caused hazards are a very real threat. They don't abide by a certain schedule. Their window of opportunity can be wide open at any time, day or night, so it's important that we take proper action in order to keep that window shut. But what can you do if the window is not shut and you notice a potential problem?

Figure 7.2 provides some problem-solving steps to consider before an incident occurs.

FIGURE 7.2: Steps in the Problem-Solving Process

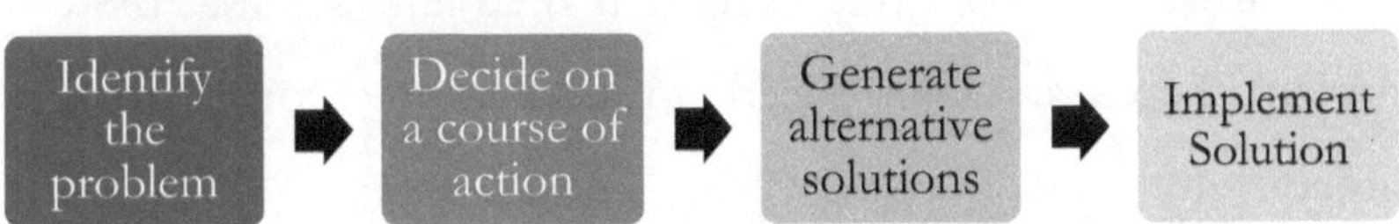

Step 1: Identify the Problem

Identifying the problem is always the first challenge you'll need to get past. After all, you are not out of the house because you are specifically searching for an individual that may potentially be an active shooter. You are out for anything from grocery shopping to getting your license renewed to lunch with a friend, or any other activity that would seem like nothing out of the ordinary. But never forget, you should remain vigilant at all times and take notice. Observe your surroundings to ensure you remain one step ahead in remaining proactive.

Once again, do not overlook the totality of circumstances. With practice, you will be able to identify irregularities and conclude whether or not your life is in danger.

Consider the following example: while shopping at a large retail store you are listening to the normal background noise from people chattering (customers, vendors, and staff) and the mellow background music playing over the store's speakers. In a split second, most of the people start running in all directions. Some are moving right past you. Many of them are screaming and you can't make out what they're saying. In many ways, this is a very uncertain situation. But if there's one thing that *is* certain, it's that there is a problem here, and you need to take some form of action immediately.

Step 2: Decide on a Course of Action

Now that you have identified there is a problem, you will need to decide on a course of action right away. This will be difficult, considering your physiological response to the situation will be one of extreme stress. But thinking with some level of clarity and coherence is essential at this point.

Step 3: Generate Alternative Solutions

Thinking of alternative solutions may be an important tactic to implement. There is a balance that you must adhere to, though. Time is of the essence and you may have little time to put together a Plan B in the heat of the moment. But brainstorming on alternative ideas to survive may come in handy if you think proactively and with a somewhat clear mindset.

Step 4: Implement Solution

Once you have decided on the course of action and a possible alternative to the matter, you must commit to that action. Do not try to gather feedback on your decision. Do not look for consensus or acceptance. Your survival is of most importance.

8

Strength in Options

"In the middle of chaos lies opportunity."

Bruce Lee

I've said this before, but it bears repeating. Having potential scenarios in your head and thinking about response options will help in selecting the best course of action. It's a mental exercise that will greatly strengthen the odds of your survival if a situation should occur.

At this point, you may have heard of "run, hide or fight" or other variations. These are solid foundational options that you can build a more effective plan upon. Just bear in mind that no matter what the plan's specifics end up being, there is a correct way to run and an effective way to hide. And *always* remember that fighting an active shooter is a high risk option that should only be used as a last resort. But with a clear head and strong sense of intuition, you should begin to "automatically" know what option will be best.

For example, sometimes you may not be able to run because the space between you and the perpetrator is too constricted. By running towards the individual, you are putting yourself in the direct line of fire and may end up getting shot. Running outside of his field of fire is much safer, but if you don't know where the individual actually is, that will offer up a whole new set of risks. Alternatively, hiding may not be the best option either, or it may just not be available at the time. If you do choose to hide, you may corner yourself into a situation without an exit or alternative route. And then there's fighting, the riskiest alternative plan of all. Always remember that a bullet is faster than your fist before you decide to do something extreme.

FIGURE 8.1: Active Shooter Management Matrix

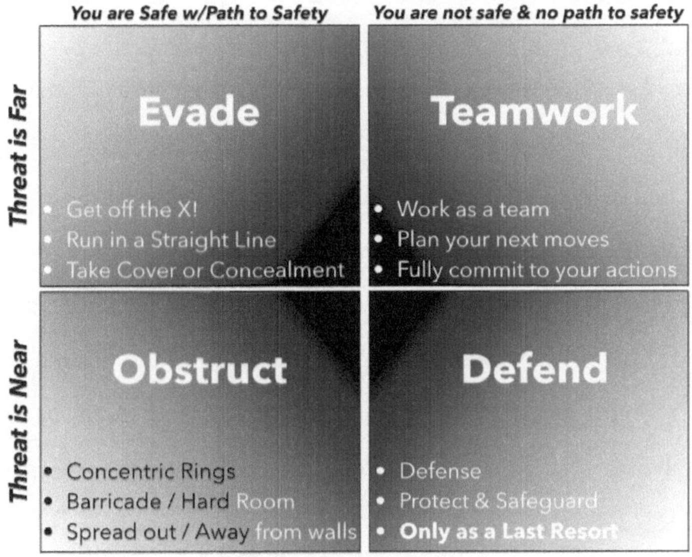

Copyright © by Fidelis NA, LLC

These alternative options should be sharpened through prior training. The more aware you are of their specifics, the better prepared you will be if a situation unfolds.

In Figure 8.1, you'll see four alternative suggestions that one may consider implementing to respond to an active shooter incident.

Evade

In the moment when you notice there is a life or death situation developing around you, you need to think with clarity and focus on the most important goal – your personal safety. As mentioned earlier, you'll need to decide on a course of action to avoid the problem, even though stress will be a seemingly insurmountable obstacle. A best practice is for you to plan an escape route as soon as you enter any location.

I like to break "escape" down into three subcategories, which are evading, eluding and dodging. By evading, we are avoiding the danger at all possible costs. By eluding, you are skillfully escaping the danger through a series of steps. By dodging the threat, you are avoiding with quick and sudden movements instead of running aimlessly into the gunfire or into an unsafe location.

Please take note that if you see a shooter or hear shooting near you, your best course of action is to run in the opposite direction from the sound of gunfire.

Get off the X!

Dangerous situations produce abnormal reactions among people. If you happen to be near an active shooter incident, you may experience fear and confusion, obviously. You may feel startled or anxious. But once you recognize that your life is in danger, you must act. The first step in taking action is to remove yourself from the location you are on. This is called "Getting off the X." The X is the location where you are standing or sitting in that particular moment. It is an incredibly dangerous spot to be in. The second you recognize the threat; you need to run from the danger without hesitation and not remain stagnant. Don't spend a second trying to make sense of what you're hearing or seeing. Just react and allow yourself to go into survival mode.

Run in a Straight Line

When running, move as fast as possible in a straight line. If you are in direct line of site of the shooter, run straight but move laterally. Run outside of the shooters "field of fire" or 10AM - 2PM (see Figure 8.2). This is the range of where the shooting may take place.

FIGURE 8.2: 10AM - 2PM Field of Fire

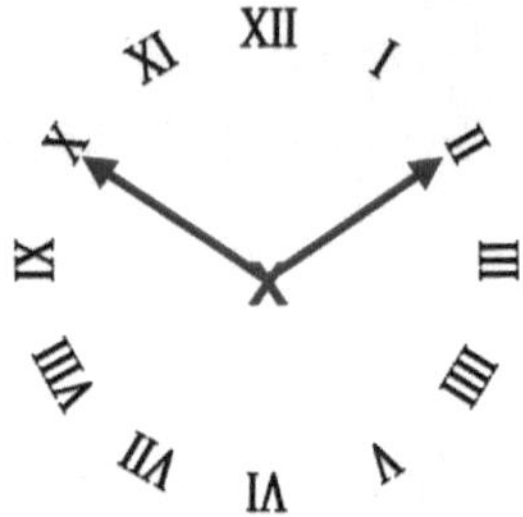

Picture of a clock displaying 10 & 2, a field of fire.
© Photo by Luis A. Ramirez

The shortest distance between two points is a straight line. Zigzagging has been seen as the best tactic here, but I'm here to tell you that it will only increase the time it takes for you to get to safety. And when a threat arises, time is not on your side.

Take Cover

Identifying cover is of vital importance in the immediate onset of a hostile act if you are unable to escape immediately. Cover can be any structure substantial enough to stop a bullet or any other dangers. Find cover that can best safeguard you from injury. A structure or item that is solid instead of hollow provides the most protection. Depending on the resources around you, try to identify items such as a telephone pole, a concrete wall, a thick table, or a car's engine block.

FIGURE 8.3: Cover and Concealment Matrix

Cover Examples (Solid Structures)	Concealment Examples (Hollow)
A Thick Table or Pool Table	Cubicles, Thin Table, etc.
A Substantial Door	Wooden Doors or fences
Concrete, metal, or iron walls	Sheetrocked Walls
A car's engine block, jersey barriers	Car Doors
Always remember, if you have an opportunity to evacuate to a safer place, do it.	

Note that there is a difference between "cover" and "concealment." Concealment is anything that will hide you visually but may not stop a bullet or other dangers. Again, situational awareness is of vital importance at all times. When entering a location, begin to scan the room for items of cover and concealment. (see Figure 8.3) As you assess your surrounding environment identify items that may be hollow such as cubicles, a thin table, wooden doors. These are items that a bullet may penetrate and present a risk and vulnerability.

Take cover as quickly as you can and hold your position. First, identify the direction of the gunfire. If you are choosing to move, do not do so when you hear the sound of gunfire. Instead, move during the pause in between gunfire.

Take cover behind a substantial object. If you notice impacts from the bullets, consider bounding from cover and move again during a pause of gunfire.

If you are outside or near vehicles, ensure you take cover behind a substantial object like the engine block of a vehicle or a jersey barrier.

Consider doing the following:

- Leave personal belongings. Your concern is to survive.
- Commit to your actions.
- Help others to escape but do not attempt to move the wounded.
- Prevent others from entering a building with an active shooter.
- Keep your hands visible for law enforcement to see.
- Follow instructions of law enforcement officers.
- Call 911 when possible.

Obstruct

Another tactic and strategy you can take is to obstruct the path of an active shooter, if you have the time to do so. Identify things near you that will help you achieve this goal. By obstructing, you are deliberately making it difficult for the shooter to advance, and therefore distract them from their train of thought. Remember, these people are on the move and have a plan they want to see through. Hindering it in any way will throw them off their game.

FIGURE 8.4: Example of a Concentric Ring of Security #2

Picture of a classroom with desks stacked up in a concentric ring formation and a heavy desk pushed on a door.
© Photo by Luis A. Ramirez

If you plan to obstruct but the shooter is too close and evacuation is not possible, find a safe area to hide and enter into a lockdown mindset. If possible, hide near an escape route. Move inside a room or office and lock it. Try to choose a location where the walls might be thicker and have fewer windows. Push heavy objects such as furniture or heavy items to block the doors. Find further cover within the room. Attempt to create extra barriers inside of the room with all the furniture or things at your disposal. (See Figure 8.4) Think of a fortress. Think of a shield. Use everything at your disposal and create extra layers to effectively obstruct the path in case the shooter attempts to penetrate the door.

Barricades

Proper utilization of barricades can serve as the difference between life and death in an active shooter crisis. The most obvious barricade is a heavy, strong door that has been securely locked. Given the standard indoor environments that typically host these types of dangerous incidents, you most likely won't have trouble finding a door that the shooter most likely won't be able to force open.

This is not to say that your typical doors can't provide you with protection. Yes, the standard doors you might find inside homes or older buildings might not be as strong as the doors we previously mentioned. Their locks might be far less complex and might not withstand a great amount of force. But you must understand that active shooters are on the move and at high alert. Attempting to unlock or perhaps even breach a door by force is unlikely, as the perpetrator has no intention of compromising their momentum.

No matter what type of door you've locked, you must reinforce the barrier whenever possible. In the case of most corporate buildings or educational facilities, there are a number of items that can be used to further barricade yourself and those around you from danger.

Hard Rooms

A "Hard Room" is any type of room that may offer you and others protection during an unexpected crisis. Think of it as a safe room or a panic room you can quickly enter and barricade. Hard rooms may, at times, be fortified or hardened structures that provide lifesaving protection. They may be designed substantially heavier and thicker than your standard type of door in order to resist forced entry and impact.

A room like this makes for an excellent place in which to avoid a shooter's path. As this book mentioned earlier, the perpetrator will be on the move. On some level, they know time is not on their side and that law enforcement has most likely been alerted. Attempting to break down a door, let alone a hard room's door, may not be of their best interest. It would only impede them.

To mitigate against the threat, conduct an assessment to determine possible hard room locations inside and outside your facility. You will have to balance your resources with the need to establish the hard room, if you do not have one. Your chances of survival may increase by improving your options to remove yourself and others from the danger by hiding, barricading, and locking yourself in the room. Through the assessment, you must determine what works best for your respective situation. Consider asking yourself the following questions:

- What is the risk of an active shooter (or other hazards) to my assets?

- What existing refuge options do I have if an active shooter (or other hazards) occur in my location?

- How feasible is it to dedicate an area or room as a hard room, and what are the potential costs?

But what if you are visiting a facility (educational or commercial environments) and you are caught in the crossfire of an active shooter, with escape not being an available option? You might not know the location of the facility's safe zones or hard rooms. But to mitigate your risk of exposure, consider identifying the location of public restrooms as you enter the facility. The restroom may provide solid foundation for your safety. Some of these doors may be much more difficult to penetrate and may be equipped with a strong deadbolt.

But first confirm that it does have a substantial door with the ability to lock securely. Also verify if it has multiple entries and exits. Confirm which way the door opens. Does it open out or into the restroom? If there are objects you can barricade the door with, use those resources to your advantage. Lastly, confirm whether or not there are windows inside the restroom. They may be utilized as an escape hatch if the danger gets closer to you. Use this logic and approach with other rooms.

Concentric Rings

The space between an active shooter and their ultimate objective is seldom one straight line that is completely free of obstructions. There are usually a number of layers in the shooter's way. Each layer represents an opportunity for the shooter to be held at bay until the situation is resolved, either by surrender, arrest, or the shooter's death. But if the shooter is freely able to pass through these rings or layers, they will move from one concentric ring of security to the next, each of them decreasing in their diameter, until you and those around you are within the same space as the shooter. These rings or layers may come in many variations, but the security between each ring should be more intense as the threat gets closer.

FIGURE 8.5: Concentric Rings of Security

Ring #	Ring Name	Outside-In	Inside Facility
Ring 1	Perimeter	Parking Lot	Close & Lock Door
Ring 2	Exterior	Perimeter of Building	Barricade w/ heavy objects
Ring 3	Interior	Inside the Building	Create layers with obstacles
Ring 4	Restricted Area	Your Door	Shield or Fortress
Ring 5	Asset	You	You

An example is as shown on Figure 8.5 while Figure 8.6 depicts the concentric rings of security. You can see that the further you are away from the perpetrator, the safer you should be.

Consider using all the resources at your disposal to strengthen the concentric rings inside of the room you are physically barricading. How do you do this? **Figure 8.7** illustrates an example of a school utilizing their desks to create an additional ring, effectively providing a shield. If possible, create additional shields behind each layer to provide minimum exposure and keep the threat at bay.

FIGURE 8.6 Concentric Rings of Security

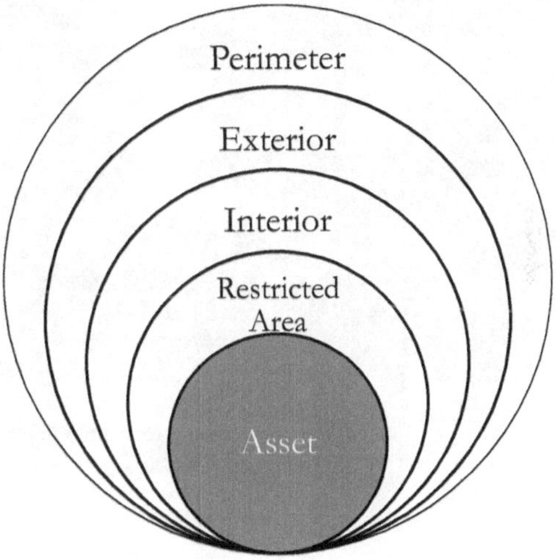

Spread Out & Stay Low

When obstructing, consider spreading out and staying low. By sitting down, you would expose your torso to the shooter and its bullets. By standing you are also exposing yourself completely. Get down to the ground in a prone position for minimum exposure behind the concentric rings you have created beforehand.

FIGURE 8.7: Example of a Concentric Ring of Security #3

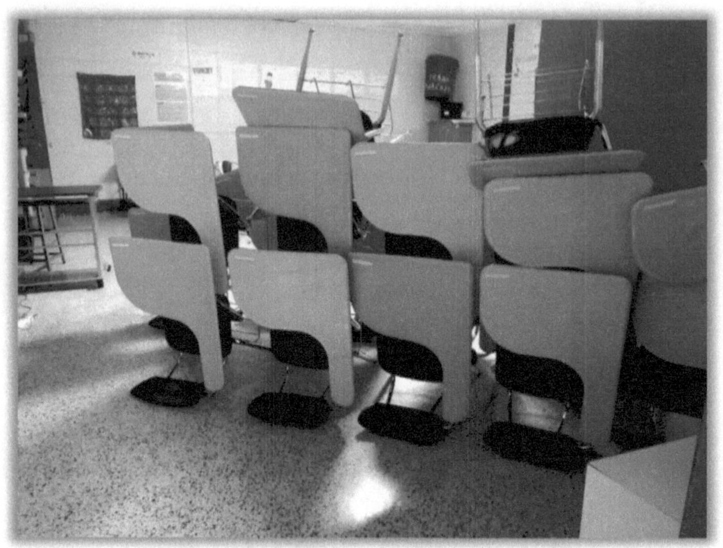

Picture of a classroom with desks stacked up in a concentric ring formation.
© Photo by Luis A. Ramirez

Stay Away from Walls

Do not lean or stand against any wall. Stay approximately six inches away from the walls during an active shooter incident. Why? If a bullet penetrates where you are located, there is a possibility the bullet may impact a wall. From that point, the bullet may traverse or travel along the wall. If you are sitting or standing near the wall, you run the risk of getting hit. If you look at how SWAT teams or highly trained military teams tactically breach into a building, they never lean on or get close to the wall. They remain aware of their surroundings and stay clear from the wall. They take special precautions so as not to be impacted by any stray bullets.

Fatal Funnel

Never take cover inside the "fatal funnel" which is located directly in front of a door (see Figure 8.8). A fatal funnel is one of the most dangerous locations a person may be exposed to during these incidents. This is a tactical concept which takes into account the path leading from the entry of a door, where a perpetrator may have advantage by pointing their weapon in the 10-2 angle. The path of their muzzle and bullet(s) will provide the angle of a fatal funnel.

FIGURE 8.8: Fatal Funnel

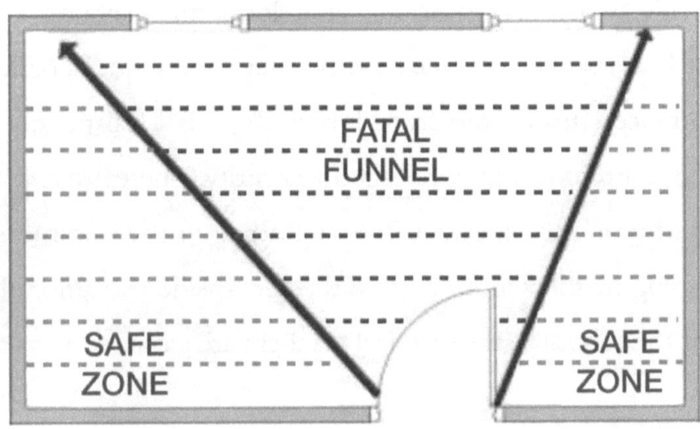

Observe the graphic shown in Figure 8.8. On the bottom you will see the door swings open inward, thus providing direct view of the inside of the room to the shooter. The red lines to the left and right depict the "field of fire" or 10AM - 2PM angles and point of view a shooter will have to aim at their target(s). The area in green is potentially the safe zone in this scenario. Aim to establish the concentric rings of security in the safe zone, but also have a backup plan in case you need to pivot from your initial strategy. Establish a robust system of layers inside the room if you do not have a safe zone inside of the room. Do nothing is not an option.

Let's consider some hypothetical examples.

Hypothetical Scenario #1

It's a Monday morning at a local high school. Campus security is doing their routine patrols around the school's parking lot and entrances. Inside the front lobby, there is local police officer assigned to provide additional school security. There are two sets of hallways beyond the lobby, with one leading to the classrooms and one leading to the school's amphitheater. Inside the amphitheater, most of the school's students and teachers are gathered for a school assembly. Two more campus security guards are standing at the main entrance to the amphitheater.

A shooter parks his car and takes an AR-15 out of the trunk. He is a student of the school and is familiar with its layout. He is also aware of the school assembly that is currently taking place.

With this information, let's identify the rings.

- Ring One: Parking lot
- Ring Two: Front lobby
- Ring Three: Hallway leading to amphitheater.
- Ring Four: Amphitheater

Each of these rings present an opportunity for the situation to be put to an end.

As the shooter advances through the parking lot, the security guards can identify the threat and radio the guards and police officer within the school. At this point, security can electronically secure and lock the front entrance, as well as any other nearby entrances the shooter can use. The officer can then radio police dispatch and assist in securing the points of entry to the school and attempt to neutralize the shooter before he has a chance to advance through the parking lot and into the building.

However, if the security guards are not at that area of the school's perimeter at the time, or if the shooter has wounded or perhaps even killed them, the shooter has a much higher chance of successfully entering the building.

Once the shooter is within the front lobby, the police officer can identify the threat and attempt to stop the shooter by force. If the shooter is able to return fire, the officer can attempt to neutralize the threat, take cover, and/or radio for backup. At this point, the situation can be resolved with the officer wounding or killing the shooter, or even overwhelming him to the point of suicide or surrender. The gunfight can also keep the shooter at bay until backup arrives and engages the shooter from his blind spot.

In the event that the shooter somehow is able to outgun the officer, or if the officer isn't where they're supposed to be in the first place, the shooter now has a clear path into the hallway leading to the amphitheater.

The shooter is now in the hallway and heading for the amphitheater's entrance. For the security guards, the only practical way to keep the shooter from advancing past this point is to secure the amphitheater's entrance from the inside by locking and/or barricading the doors. This should impede the shooter long enough for law enforcement to arrive.

If the security guards fail to do this, the shooter now has the opportunity to enter into the innermost ring. The potential number of casualties is now at its highest point. The survival of the individuals within the amphitheater now depends on their ability to either escape, obstruct and barricade with concentric rings of security inside other rooms or in the amphitheater, or physically overpower the shooter (if this is their only choice).

Hypothetical Scenario #2

It is 2:50 p.m. on a Wednesday and the routine marketing meeting is wrapping up at the company headquarters. The meeting is held on the 2nd floor see-through conference room which staff refer to as "The Fishbowl." From the room, the attendees have direct sight of the main entrance. The meeting has not started yet and 25 people are eagerly looking forward to moving on with their day.

Meanwhile, the main entrance vestibule is jammed with a group of 10 visitors from out of town. The security guard, Pat, is caught off-guard with the influx of people. Pat immediately tries to manage the situation by accounting for each individual before the guest sponsor arrives. The sponsor is expected to escort the group to the Fishbowl for the 3:30 p.m. meeting.

While the visitors and Pat wait for the sponsor, a bottleneck has developed and regular staff members cannot enter the building as efficiently as usual. This bottleneck has left the front door completely open while the visitors impede the entry and continue their respective conversations. The regular employees cannot easily access the scanner located inside the vestibule due to the jammed entry way. The guard remotely opens the interior door for the regular employees without fully validating their identity nor requiring each employee to swipe their badge.

Meanwhile a suspicious person has been sitting in his car since the lunch rush-hour observing and analyzing the front entrance pattern unfolding. It is now 2:53 p.m. and this was his opportunity to put the plan in motion. He walks toward the trunk of his car and dons his tactical vest and his weapon. He aggressively jogs toward the weakest point – the front door. He points his weapon towards the individuals holding the exterior door and then to the people near the entrance door. He runs up the stairs towards The Fishbowl.

The shooter was not challenged by any of the people or systems put into place and he continues to aim at his targets inside the Fishbowl. It is now 2:58 p.m. He assumes law enforcement is on their way.

With this information, let's identify the rings and best practices.

- Ring One: Outer Layer (Perimeter, Grounds, Parking lot)
- Ring Two: Vestibule / Outside door (Building Perimeter)
- Ring Three: Inside Layer (The guard door)
- Ring Four: Interior Layer (Rooms, Areas, Containers)

The shooter was sitting in his car for a substantial amount of time. Watching. Observing. Loading his magazines. No roaming securing personnel challenged the individual, nor did the security booth have the capability to view the CCTV cameras for suspicious activity. Had the guard uncovered what was going on in the parking lot, Pat may have had the time to react proactively.

Another best practice would be for the security guards to have knowledge of large parties and the details of their arrival. This would have enabled Pat to escort the group to a secured waiting area as a method of crowd control. However, the vulnerability allowed the perpetrator ample time to breach the perimeter door and gain access to the core assets of the company.

The guard's decision to unlock the interior door (via the maglock door by-pass) without identifying staff badges also created another vulnerability. All of this happened throughout the course of roughly 0:45 seconds. It was too late for anyone in the Fishbowl to react accordingly and the potential number of casualties is now at its highest point.

The survival of personnel on the first and second floor depends on their decision, capability, and ability to get off their X and exit the building in the opposite direction of the sound of gunfire, create hard rooms with barriers inside of the building, or physically defend if the need arises.

Defend and Take Action

"The important thing is to strive towards a goal which is not immediately visible. That goal is not the concern of the mind, but of the spirit."

Flight of Arras, Antoine de Saint-Exupéry

Defense

As previously mentioned, each of the concentric rings of security are separated by potential barriers of one kind or another that can either impede or possibly even put an end to the advancement of a threat such as an active shooter. As we have seen lately in businesses open to pedestrians, active shooters have shown a pattern. They are able to reach their intended target(s) without much resistance. For example, on August 3, 2019 a perpetrator walked into a Walmart shopping center in El Paso, Texas to conduct reconnaissance on the amount of people inside the store. He then proceeded to his car to don his body armor and grab his weapons. The perpetrator reentered the Walmart without resistance and proceeded with his plan. He had full ability to penetrate each layer of security and reach the intended target. (Bill Hutchinson, 2019) & (O'Kane, 2019)

Conversely, on August 9, 2019 yet another incident occurred at a separate Walmart shopping center in Springfield, Missouri. The perpetrator was parked outside the Walmart and grabbed his body armor from the trunk. He then casually grabbed a shopping cart and walked into the Walmart carrying a loaded rifle and handgun but was stopped immediately by an off-duty fire fighter. (The Associated Press, 2019)

These two examples illustrate scenarios where (1) you may not be able to stop an individual from carrying out his intended plans and (2) where you may find yourself in a position to decide and stop an individual before they pursue with his or her intended plan. If you find yourself in close proximity to an active shooter, and you are within an arm's length of the perpetrator, you may have to make a though choice. But this choice should be as a last resort or only option. You will need to intelligently resist an attack by protecting, guarding, or safeguarding yourself and others from danger.

Just keep in mind, you always have options.

Attack

Fighting back should always be considered a last resort, and it must be your own decision. This point cannot be stressed enough.

If you attack impulsively, irresponsibly, or without full commitment to your decision, you can actually make the situation worse and decrease the odds of your survival, as well as the survival of those around you. Therefore, it is absolutely crucial that you think before you act, and ultimately see your actions through. Fight aggressively and defend yourself.

Weapons

If you have the opportunity to grab an item near you that can be thrown and used to defend yourself or distract the shooter, do it. When you picture a weapon, your mind most likely goes to a gun or knife of some kind. In actuality, there are a number of everyday objects that can be used to incapacitate a perpetrator. These items may be heavy items, sharp items, or even hot liquids. Items that you are able to throw can prove both effective and safe. The goal here is to distract, disable, and disorient the perpetrator. Harming them isn't necessarily priority one. For instance, if you can pick a paperweight off a desk and whip it at the perpetrator, you've just interrupted his thought process and thrown his focus off. Now, if you were accurate enough to hit him right between the eyes, consider that a bonus.

"Meat & Metal"

Before I go deeper into the concept of physically engaging a shooter, I want to reiterate that fighting should always be considered a last resort and it must be your own decision. But if you must engage an active shooter, the "head-on" approach is not to be used. Obviously, approaching the perpetrator from the front puts you at extreme risk of being shot, even if you happen to be armed yourself. Instead, try to approach from the side or rear. The key is to avoid the shooter's field of vision and field of fire.

If you're able to get within arm's length of the shooter by approaching them from the side or rear, the next step is to take control. An effective tactic is what's called "meat and metal," with the meat being the perpetrator's forearm or hand, and the metal being the barrel of the weapon. The goal here is not to disarm the perpetrator. They may very well react wildly and shoot indiscriminately once they feel threatened. To reduce the likelihood of these wild shots hitting anyone, you must grab the barrel of the weapon and push upwards while securing your grip on the forearm.

Work as a Team

As we've seen from the examples previously cited in this book, shooters act alone, statistically. Therefore, those who find themselves in an incident have one advantage that the shooter does not: strength in numbers.

In order to make the most of this advantage, teamwork is key. You and your group may be able to plan out your attack. Chances are, however, that time will not be on your side, and discussing a plan while a shooter is in the room may draw attention.

The key to a group attack is the same as when one tries to take a shooter down alone. Approach from the side or back and commit fully to your actions. Everyone in the group needs to move fast and hard, with zero hesitation. The group attack should be made up of a flurry of strikes to overpower the shooter, as well as the "meat and metal" technique on a group level in order to keep others from being on the receiving end of the weapon. Please note, the perpetrators gun must not be touched if it is laying on the floor. Do not attempt to pick up the weapon. It will create a safety hazard and may contaminate the crime scene.

Positive Mental Attitude

Simply put, an active shooter is a terrorist. They are there to create terror, fear, anxiety, confusion, etc. If you decide it's time to act, commit to your actions with a positive mental attitude. There may be a period of a "fog of war," where your certainty and precision will not be at its best. However, speed and agility can make up for that loss. Adopt a fighter mentality, just like Kendrick Castillo did when he fought the perpetrator aggressively and heroically on May 7, 2019 at the STEM School Highlands Ranch in Colorado (Yan, 2019). The same goes for Riley Howell, who also fought the perpetrator aggressively and heroically at the University of North Carolina at Charlotte on April 30, 2019. (Fieldstadt, 2019)

Stress Management

Finding yourself in the midst of an active shooting incident is, without a shadow of a doubt, one of the most harrowing and traumatic situations that a human being can experience.

Every man, woman and child who are thrust into this danger will experience a sharp increase in both physiological and psychological stress. Even experienced combat veterans face these intense emotions. The goal is not to eliminate these feelings entirely.

In fact, that would be next to impossible. There is no such thing as stress elimination, only stress management.

Physiological Response

Understanding how your body will react under extreme pressure will help manage any stress you might experience. There are certain ways your body will react in accordance to the stress level it's experiencing.

It is normal to feel stress. We are built to feel it and wired to manage its different levels. When we are suddenly affected by abnormal circumstances that stress us out beyond your control, your body goes into a fight or flight mode. This is your body's way of telling you that you must do something about this situation in order to keep yourself safe.

As with all reactions, understanding what they are is the first step in managing them. According to the Mayo Clinic, the section of your brain known as the hypothalamus sets off an alarm system in your body via a combination of nerve and hormone signals. This system stimulates your adrenal glands, which are located atop your kidneys. This will release a surge of hormones, mainly adrenaline and cortisol. (Staff, 2019)

Adrenaline increases your heart rate, elevates your blood pressure and escalates your energy supplies. Cortisol, on the other hand, the primary stress hormone, increases sugars (glucose) in the bloodstream, enhances your brain's use of glucose and increases the availability of substances that repair tissues. (Ibid)

FIGURE 8.9: Physiological Effects

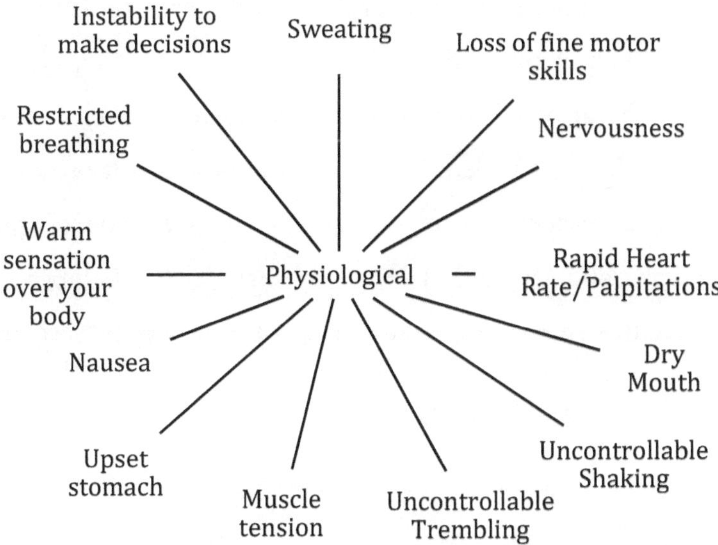

Cortisol also curbs functions that could be detrimental in a fight-or-flight situation. It alters immune system responses and suppresses the digestive system, the reproductive system and growth processes. This complex natural alarm system also communicates with the brain regions that control mood, motivation and fear. (Ibid)

Your goal is to manage the stress and any physiological barrier you are experiencing and improve high risk decision making. We should not allow our brain's impulsive reactions to completely override our decision-making processes.

You may experience the following physiological responses during heightened levels of stress, which I've depicted on the graphic shown in Figure 8.9.

Understanding how your body will react under extreme stress will help you manage the physiological effects you will experience. Your body's physiological and perceptual responses will be elevated during a violent event. Whether you like it or not, your body will react according to the stress level its experiencing. First Responders and Armed Forces Special Elite members also experience this stress. Perpetrators are not immune to these effects either.

Perceptual Effects

You may need to snap out of perceptual effects, such as tunnel vision, auditory exclusion, or time distortion. During tunnel vision, your sight will become distorted, making it so objects cannot be properly seen. If you are experiencing auditory exclusion, you are having temporary loss of hearing due to high stress. As such it is in the same family as tunnel vision, both of which present that feeling of the slowing of time in the mind. Essentially, time distortion is defined as an effect that makes the passage of time feel difficult to keep track of.

The first step to managing your stress is to prepare in advance mentally and know how your body will react. In the event of a hostile attack, your immediate reaction could save your life. If you are hiding, or have time to think, take multiple deep breaths, stay positive, and commit to your actions with confidence.

Optimal Efficiency

To reach optimal efficiency, you may need to utilize a breathing technique known as "Box Breathing" or "Tactical Breathing." Box Breathing is a useful tool for regulating your stress, calming yourself down, and keeping a clear head. The technique is frequently used by military and law enforcement personnel, which serves as a testament to just how effective it can be.

Box Breathing is comprised of a simple four-second rotation that includes breathing in, holding your breath, breathing out, and holding it once more as shown in Figure 8.10. The process is to be repeated again and again, with no breaks in between.

FIGURE 8.10: Box Breathing

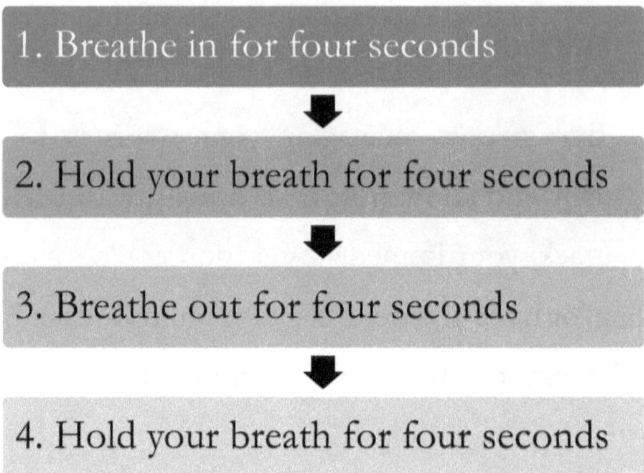

Practice this technique on your own. If done correctly, you'll notice a drop in your anxiety and an increase of focus. It might seem hard to believe, but this simple tool can substantially boost your odds of survival. Again, the first step to managing your stress is to be mentally prepared in advance.

9

Control the Bleeding

*"The only thing more tragic than a death from bleeding…is
a death that could have been prevented.."*

The American College of Surgeons

Before we delve into this next chapter, let me be perfectly clear: I am not a doctor. I am not a nurse. But I am a Marine, and as such, I was taught these life saving techniques that can be used to treat gunshot victims. If you use these techniques, you must do so with great care. Consult with a physician if you have time to do so.

According to the American College of Surgeons, a victim who is bleeding from an artery can die in as little as three minutes. (The American College of Surgeons, n.d.) This is the most dangerous type of bleeding and it is known as hemorrhaging. Hemorrhaging is the 2nd leading cause of death (30% to 40%) when bleeding from an artery. (Eric R. Donley, 2019) As you know, arteries are blood vessels which carry oxygen-rich blood from the heart, so it is important to have a game plan to help save a person bleeding profusely. It is typically seen with massive or deep wounds.

Having a basic knowledge of how to control the bleeding is crucial. The first step you need to take is to assess the situation. If you see a person bleeding as a result of a gunshot from an active shooter event, your top priority is to control the bleeding. You must do all that you can to make sure the person is able to tell their story once this horrific event has come to a conclusion.

Yes, the paramedics and police are most likely on their way. But if you can help yourself or if you can help others, you basically have three minutes before it's too late. As we have seen, it takes an average of three to five minutes for police to arrive on the scene and handle the situation. Consider all the duties they have during these scenarios, though. They must secure the perimeter, set up barricades, and possibly even neutralize or arrest the shooter. On top of all that, it is critical that they control the flow of people, and that includes the paramedics.

By the time the paramedics make it to the wounded, it may be too late. You may need to take control of the situation until they arrive. If this is the case, adhere to these four basic steps: restore the breathing, control the bleeding, treat for shock, and protect the wound.

The inherent danger of these wounds is the chance of the victim bleeding to death. So, to control the bleeding memorize the THREAT acronym that I've listed below. This acronym is a method of prioritization that was articulated by the American College of Surgeons and key federal partners at the Hartford Consensus Conference on April 2, 2013. (Joint Committee to Create a National Policy to Enhance Survivability from Intentional Mass Casualty Shooting Events, 2013) The aim here is to create a strategy on how to respond to the challenges you may face if you are attempting to treat a wounded shooting victim.

1. Threat suppression
2. Hemorrhage control
3. Rapid extrication to safety
4. Assessment by medical providers
5. Transport to definitive care

You will most likely just deal with the first and the second. The paramedics will ensure steps three to five are fulfilled, but you must help with suppressing the threat and controlling the bleeding.

In the event there is someone wounded, the victims of gunfire will face one or more of the following five wounds that I've listed below. Four are "open wounds" and one is a "closed wound." You can use the acronym CALIP (Crush, Abrasion, Laceration, Incision and Puncture) to help memorize each wound category.

Closed Wounds

The first is a closed wound known as a "crush." The wound is caused by an overwhelming action or a severe blow to a portion of the body. These wounds pose a high risk for infection.

We've all had a bruise, but what is a bruise, exactly? Well, when your body is struck with a blunt object, the tissues beneath the skin are crushed. Hence, the bruise or contusion. Remember, these wounds are not open and bleeding, therefore they are categorized as closed wounds. Reflect back on a horrible bruise you may have experienced. Did you swell? That's typical of these injuries, since blood fills within the wound itself.

Open Wounds

The second wound is known as an "abrasion." It is an open wound that is caused when the skin is rubbed off. It poses a high probability of foreign objects entering the wound, which increases chance of infection. When your skin is peeled or shaved from your body in this manner, your blood may look as though it is oozing.

But if a sharp object pierces your skin, it creates what is known as a "laceration." Depending on its severity, it can damage body tissue, muscle, nerves and/or blood vessels. These wounds are caused by a tearing of the skin rather than a cutting.

"Incisions" are in the same family as lacerations but are much more precise. They are not caused by jagged edges, but rather straight and sharp ones, which create a clean cut across the skin.

Pointed objects that go straight into the skin result in "puncture" wounds. These are caused by nails, knives, a gunshot or any other pointed object. These wounds are typically smaller than the other types, which presents a less severe form of external bleeding. However, the result is a great deal of internal damage.

Be careful with these wounds since the true extent of the damage cannot be seen with the naked eye. Wait for medical help.

Treatment of Open Wounds

If you do see an open wound, the clock is ticking. Try to apply direct pressure and use pressure dressing or a tourniquet to help the person through the ordeal. Also note that the wound may not be sterilized, therefore you may run the risk of contamination or infection.

To help the casualty and mitigate the risk of infection or contamination, apply an emergency bandage (Israeli bandage) or a gauze as quickly as possible, but do so with caution. If you apply a bandage with unnecessary tightness, it can result in even more damage because you are restricting the blood flow to the lower extremities. Alternatively, if the bandage is loosely applied it can cause the dressing to fall out of place. Aim to apply the bandage snugly. Note: an Israeli bandage provides excellent results and can be self-administered.

After you successfully apply the bandage (to yourself or another person), you want to assess the condition and the person. Confirm that the individual or yourself are not feeling any tingling, numbness or pain, and keep an eye out for discoloring skin. These are all indicators of poor circulation, which may be a sign of a tight bandage. To mitigate against tightness, aim to leave the fingers and toes uncovered. Doing so will help you monitor any potential changes in color.

To reduce further serious bleeding, aim to keep the injury elevated and immobilized.

Serious Bleeding

If you do not have a bandage available at the time, use the resources you have at your disposal – your hands. Applying pressure to the wound with your hands may seriously increase the risk of infection, but in those first crucial moments, you need to control the bleeding to the best of your ability.

Utilize Pressure Points

As an alternative, you can apply compression to a pressure point to control the loss of blood. Humans have 22 pressure points in total. The following three points are the most important. The first point is known as the brachial (arm), the second is the femoral (upper thigh), and the third is the carotid (neck) arteries. By applying pressure to these arteries, you may be able to control the bleeding more efficiently than you would from applying direct pressure to the wound. Remember to apply pressure to these points with the heel of your palm and push downward toward the bone. Continue doing so until the bleeding has been controlled.

Tourniquet

A tourniquet should be used as a last resort if the arm or leg is bleeding. Only apply the tourniquet if the bandage did not work efficiently, the manual pressure failed, and the artery pressure was unsuccessful. Why? Because a tourniquet may present permanent damage.

The tourniquet should be placed one to two inches above the open wound. You can use two or three of your fingers to measure this but be sure to document the time you have wrapped a tourniquet, a belt, or a cloth material such as a shirt. Write the time anywhere with a permanent marker. On the person's forehead, near the tourniquet, wherever you can. But write it clearly so the paramedics know the exact time. The goal here is to buy the person time and reduce the loss of blood. By writing the time of application, you are enabling the emergency crew and law enforcement to prioritize the wounded.

I must reiterate and let me be perfectly clear: I am not a doctor. I am not a nurse. But I am a Marine, and as such, I was taught these life saving techniques that can be used to treat gunshot victims. If you use these techniques, you must do so with great care. Consult with a physician if you have time to do so.

For additional information, please visit the Save a Life, Stop the Bleeding booklet located at the following link. (The American College of Surgeons, 2017)

https://www.bleedingcontrol.org/-
/media/bleedingcontrol/files/stop-the-bleed-booklet.ashx

10

My Final Thoughts

"One of the hardest decisions you'll ever face in life is choosing whether to walk away or try harder."

Anonymous

The overall purpose of this book is not to offer solutions to the crisis our nation is currently facing with mass shootings or active shooter incidents. It's a divisive issue with two clashing ideologies, each of them made up of people who steadfastly and passionately defend their point of view. Each must be respected.

But the will to survive in an immediate crisis eclipses those points of view. There are no societal debates during a mass shooter or an active shooter situation. It's about survival and my hope is that one person reads this book and is empowered with the tools he or she needs to survive an incident if they are literally caught in the crossfire.

I will never forget the phone call I received from one of my clients on May 13, 2019.

"Luis, Johnston-Hopkins Elementary was on a real lockdown for nearly two-hours. It was not a drill. A Police Officer came inside the building and setup a command center to observe the person whom they were negotiating with." My heart dropped as I heard more of the details. I was speechless and had many questions. But it was not the right time to probe on the matter. Everyone was safe, which is always the main priority. Fortunately, the children had lunch before the 2-hour standoff, and the individual who barricaded himself inside a house across the street from the school was taken into custody without no shots fired. (KATC News, 2019)

This incident made me more aware of the severity of an active shooter threat because I was at Johnston-Hopkins Elementary school the week prior. I was contracted to conduct risk mitigation services through my company Fidelis NA, LLC. The scope of work included physical safety and security vulnerability assessment throughout the entire campus. I remembered every detail of a 4-hour walkthrough, in which I interacted with the courteous staff and innocent children. Although the Police had a heavy presence at the school, all I could seem to think about were the results of the assessment, namely the risks and location of each vulnerability.

In this new era, lockdown drills have become as normal as conducting fire drills. The liability for not rehearsing active shooter drills is too large. To mitigate risk, school districts have begun to discuss the matter with their communities, no matter how difficult those discussions may be. The probability of an attack is low, but that doesn't eliminate the possibility for an event to occur.

The unfortunate part is that children and parents often think about these incidents in a way that is based solely in fear. My eleven-year-old daughter recently shared her fear of being a victim after watching recent news stories and listening to radio interviews. A recent survey conducted by The Children's Defense Fund showed how valid her fears just might be, as it concluded that "a shooting happening in my school" is the 2nd ranked fear of students aged 6-17, while "a shooting happening at my child's school" is the 3rd ranked fear for parents. Given the rise of mass shooting and the need for preparedness, school districts have made a conscious effort to ensure their schools go through lockdown drills as a means to provide a certain level of preparedness to children and staff. (Children's Defense Fund, 2018)

It is worth noting that entities must continuously assure they are prepared to absorb the risks, dangers, and threats of an active shooter by having a plan to manage a crisis. These entities include schools, universities, businesses, and any other organizations.

But why should organizations and the people who work or visit them fear for their lives in the first place? It seems, perhaps, society pressures each entity for continuous improvement on how they will protect their most valued asset: human beings. Entities try their best to mitigate uncertainty by investing in systems and processes, but as data show, it's sometimes not enough. More is needed. But for some reason, leaders and financial gatekeepers don't rationalize why an investment that may help their own is good for business.

I wonder, is it worth it to consider adding corporate social responsibility in the conversation? How can we learn from previous incidents?

Corporate Social Responsibility

The rise of capitalism is one of the greatest aspects of what makes the history of the United States of America so fascinating. Since the founding of the United States, the majority of people faced a new world that was liberated from British rule. They were on their own to resolve any problem, be it social or economic. This new "freedom" meant a lot of uncertainty and gave birth to unique new issues and problems that people were responsible for on some level or another.

Although it may have been challenging to live through these times, I think this period offered tremendous room to test one's ideas to solve problems and challenges faced by citizens. Without a doubt, it was a good time to be ambitious, and to prove to the world that you were hungry for change full of desire. You were able to pursue problem solving in a new world filled with a mixture of social-economic and political issues.

As people started their entrepreneurship journey to make life better through solving problems, new problems arose from fixing the initial problems.

Consider the influx of people into New York City (NYC) throughout history. As people continuously moved into NYC, the demand for basic goods and services followed pace. Hence, many businesses were established to meet the new demands of people. This supply and demand cycle still continue across the United States to this day.

Businesses must remain contemporary to satisfy the needs and demands of their consumers. On top of that, citizens continue to face increased social economic problems as well. But this rise in meeting the demands of the economy brings with it the responsibility to ensure there is a sustainable fabric incorporated into the business itself.

Or there should be, at least.

Let's look at how the International Chamber of Commerce (ICC) defined this responsibility. "The ICC says that Corporate Social Responsibility (CSR) is 'the voluntary commitment by businesses to manage their roles in society in a responsible way', and the European Union Commission says, that CSR is 'essentially a concept whereby companies decide voluntarily to contribute to a better society and cleaner environment' and more precisely, 'a concept whereby companies integrate social and environmental concerns in their business operations and in their interaction with their stakeholders on a voluntary basis'." (Mullerat, 2010)

Obviously, without customers, businesses would not survive. It would be difficult, if not impossible, to sustain their operations and market accordingly. Hence, in today's customer driven business world, consumers are more socially conscience than ever before. Businesses need to ensure they connect with their customers through socially driven topics. Although corporate social responsibility is voluntary, it's absolutely worth the effort.

Consumers want to know where they are spending their hard-earned money and what the company stands for. They also want to know who the company does business with. Who are their suppliers, their vendors, where are they sourcing their materials from? believe it or not, this stuff matters. The ethical practices of all key players is crucial, all the way up and down the supply chain.

Employees, on the other hand, want to know who exactly they are working for and if they stand for the betterment of the world at large. A company's image is one of their most valuable assets. If a company is not in tune with the image it is putting out to the public, it may face an uphill battle to retain or acquire new business.

Let's take the sneaker company TOMS as an example. If you happen to log onto their website during the month of August 2019, the first image you may have saw was their socially conscience mission and vision titled "Stand for Tomorrow." (Figure 10.1)

Within the promotion they had six social issues their customers can support: equality, access to clean water, fighting poverty, treating mental health, providing people shoes, and ending gun violence. It's all right there in their corporate motto: "With every TOMS purchase, you stand with us on issues that matter."

FIGURE 10.1: TOMS Stand for Tomorrow Website Screenshot

TOMS' approach to broad social issues is commendable. When a customer purchases one pair of sneakers, another pair is given to a child in need.

TOMS' was socially conscious of the problems many unfortunate children face worldwide. There are many children walking around the world living without adequate footwear, greatly impacting their quality of life.

A pair of sneakers can potentially ensure a child walks to school every day, or enable them to help their family obtain resources such as food or water. These are social problems shareholders, employees, and customers have expressed their opinion on and companies such as TOMS have heard them loud and clear.

One of their new initiatives is called "End Gun Violence Together." TOMS has engaged with the community by encouraging people to send a postcard asking to introduce universal background checks to their representatives in Congress. Their goal is to send one million postcards, and as of this writing they have sent 700,000.

TOMS has also invested $5 million in grants to help with prevention, intervention, and survivor support. The grants will be utilized by nonprofit organizations that have the expertise and resources needed to help end gun violence. (TOMS, n.d.)

Another example is Microsoft. Arguably one of the most recognized and successful business stories the world has ever known. Microsoft is based in Seattle and has drawn in a large and talented pool of engineers into that city's metropolitan area. The influx of engineers into the Seattle area meant great opportunities for some, but not others. For example, software engineers enjoyed high paying jobs while the salary of non-software engineers did not quite match the high paying jobs. This pay scale imbalance created a housing problem.

The problem is that with the growth and success of Microsoft, housing values increased by nearly fifty percent in the area from 2010 to 2018. Then the Amazon headquarters came into the mix, and you can easily see how the housing values jumped even higher. This is a problem.

Both companies (any company for that matter) need the support of their workers to function their operations. And of course, these workers need a place to live. So, to help solve this social problem, Microsoft has pledged to invest $500 million to "directly address the inequality that has spread in areas where the industry is concentrated, particularly on the west coast. It will fund construction for homes affordable not only to the company's own non-tech workers, but also for teachers, firefighters and other middle- and low-income residents." (Weise, 2019) In order to remain competitive and attract additional customers, Microsoft implemented a very interesting strategy to support the housing area at large.

But if we speak more about the social problems we face today, such as active shooter and mass shooting incidents, can something be done to help society in a corporately responsible way? I myself am optimistic.

Let's consider some gun control initiatives that have been implemented by several large U.S. retail companies in a socially responsible way. Consider this: if the gun can be traced to the retail store, the implications may reverberate throughout its consumers in a negative connotation.

Take Dick's Sporting Goods Inc. as an example. Dick's stopped selling assault-style rifles in all its stores after the Sandy Hook incident and has modified its policy once again following the response that high powered weapons brought to the conversation. (Jones, 2018) The Marjory Stoneman Douglas High School incident in Parkland, Florida rocked the nation once again, and Dick's did something, whether you agree with it or not.

Ed Stack, the chairman and chief executive of Dick's said, "I think CEOs today or companies today have to sit down, and they have to say what is the right thing that we should do." This influenced Dick's executives to consider having an internal conversation on what can be done to help control the risk of selling guns. Their executives decided to update Dick's policies and business model in the wake of Parkland. This change was "unanimous that Dick's should do this and stand up and take a stand." Dick's internal business operations effectively "raised the gun-buying age to 21 and end sales of assault-style rifles." (Nassauer, 2018)

And then there's Walmart. Doug McMillon, the chief executive of Walmart addressed what his company will focus on during the earnings call on August 15, 2019. Mr. McMillon provided insight to what Walmart has done in the past and what it will do going forward in a corporate socially responsible way to "strengthen its processes, improve its technology, and create an even safer environment in its stores." (Danziger, 2019) Here is a list of five initiatives Walmart will adhere to, according to Mr. McMillon (Walmart Inc., 2019):

1. Walmart stopped selling handguns in every state but Alaska in the mid 90's.
2. Walmart stopped selling military-style rifles such as the AR-15 in 2015.
3. Walmart raised the age limit to purchase a firearm or ammunition to 21 in 2018.

4. Walmart only sells a firearm after receiving a "green light" on a background check, regardless of the timeframe needed to procure that information. Federal law only requires the absence of a "red light" after three business days.

5. Walmart videotapes the point of sale for firearms, only allow certain associates to sell firearms, and secure firearms in a locking case with individual locks, among other measures.

Kroger, the nation's largest supermarket chain, is another example of how a company can take their own initiatives to help with gun control. As stated by a Kroger spokesman, "recent events demonstrate the need for additional action on the part of responsible gun retailers." The Parkland incident sparked conversations within Kroger's executive ranks, who stated that "in response to the tragic events in Parkland and elsewhere, Kroger has taken a hard look at their policies and procedures for firearm sales." (Gajanan, 2018)

Kroger announced it will "stop selling firearms to people under the age of 21 at its Fred Meyer locations" following the Parkland incident as well. (Haddon, 2018) Kroger also "raised the minimum age to buy firearms and ammunition" in addition to "stopping the selling of assault-style rifles at its Fred Meyer stores in Oregon, Washington and Idaho several years ago, and will stop accepting special orders of those kinds of weapons in Alaska, a spokesperson said in a statement." (Gajanan, 2018)

No matter where you stand on the political line, large retailers have a vested interest in assuring the products they are selling are sold responsibly. There is an issue in society nowadays with military style grade weapons being in the hands of non-military personnel. It seems that more pressure is being felt to improve how the nation manages what I believe is the root cause of mass shootings…the ammunition and weapon itself.

Here is another example why, in Mr. Stack's words, "it's OK to have differing views as long as you can have a rational and cerebral conversation about it." (Nassauer, 2018) The need to find a balanced solution and conversation comes on the aftermath of August 14, 2019. The city of Philadelphia was paralyzed for nearly eight-hours following a very strenuous and long gun battle/standoff with its city law enforcement officers. The Philadelphia Police were in the middle of serving a narcotic warrant to a felon when the operation turned sideways. The suspect barricaded himself with an automatic rifle and a enough ammunition to last nearly half a day, all by himself.

It can be debated that people are the cause of the problem. But if individuals did not have the means to acquire military style weapons, then it would obviously decrease their use among those individuals.

The impact to the city resources and the wounded police officers was immediately felt by the authorities, and the mayor sternly conveyed his opinion on the heavily loaded subject, saying he was "a little angry about someone having all that weaponry and all that firepower." (Faith Karimi, 2019)

The Need for Academic Research

In the final pages of this book, I will offer a final proposal that may potentially help uncover explanations to this national crisis.

There have been numerous perpetrators that have been arrested following these active shooting incidents. These individuals are still alive and in confinement. Taking this into consideration, continued academic research should be conducted to identify comprehensively 1) what were the reasons for the threat, 2) why did they do it, 3) what motivated them to carry their plans out, 4) what kind of preparations were conducted, 5) how did they commit to the actions, and 6) could something or someone have helped to prevent the incident from occurring? These people can be a resource in achieving this, and this all might facilitate an understanding to help other individuals that are at risk of attempting similar crimes in the future.

The proposal would analyze previous active shooters to understand their motives beyond what has been reported through government agencies, police departments and the media. The data that may be generated through the research could prove invaluable for the development of comprehensive preparedness. This data would provide researchers, policy makers, and organizations the working knowledge they would need in order to mitigate the risks associated with a potential active shooter incident.

Arguably, mental health is a typical "reason" that is provided to try to explain why a person may have conducted a crime related to an active shooter. But if we instead reflect more on the planning that is undertaken by these perpetrators beforehand, then wouldn't such an intensely challenging endeavor as trying to understand all the complex intricacies of mental health be bypassed by more tangible information? The United States Secret Service (USSS) reported, that these perpetrators typically plan their crimes "over a period of time, and the attackers often elicit concern from the people around them, therefore there exists an opportunity to stop these incidents before they occur." (U.S. Secret Service, 2019) The USSS has also stressed that, "mental illness, alone, is not a risk factor for violence, and most violence is committed by individuals who are not mentally ill."

We can fight this, if we stay aware.

Appendix A: Compilation of Lists

This appendix is an overview of each list with Your Options. You can utilize it to 1) choose different topics of interest, 2) as a point of reference, or 3) as a directory of lists.

Mental Safety Checklist to Consider Throughout Your Day (Chapter 1)

1. Has the flow of people increased or decreased?
2. Compare how people are dressed. Is there anyone that stands out?
3. Observe the pace of walk. Does anybody stand out?
4. Are the sounds you're listening to typical in relation to your setting?
5. Have things changed in the physical security of the property, such as doors being unlocked, left ajar, or pried open?
6. Do you know your exit route or exit doors?
7. Do you spot abnormal behavior?
8. Is anyone following you?

Six Examples of Physical Security Features
(Chapter 1)

1. Barriers
2. Physical security resources
3. Technology
4. Access control
5. Escort
6. Safety protocols

Ten Characteristics of Proactive People
(Chapter 2)

1. They are empowered to make a choice.
2. They plan, so they are prepared to act before they are in danger.
3. They consider possible scenarios and anticipate what may happen before it happens.
4. They keep an organized list of some kind.
5. They take the initiative, identify, and analyze risks while staying aware of their respective consequences.
6. They are engaged and have a mental picture of how to solve a problem (a response roadmap).

7. They have the foresight and can anticipate situations (danger, incidents, crisis) before they occur.

8. They rehearse preventative measures.

9. They act and do not procrastinate.

10. They hold themselves accountable.

Proactiveness Equation

(Chapter 2)

$$P^1 = \frac{(P^2 + C + P^3) * (P^4 + L + E^1 + E^2 + T) * (SA + DM)}{ToC}$$

PCP (Refer to Figure 2.2) **PLEET** (Refer to Figure 2.3)

Where:
P^1 = Proactive
P^2 = Perception
C = Comprehension
P^3 = Projection
P^4 = People
L = Location
E^1 = Event
E^2 = Environment
T = Time
SA = Self-Awareness
DM = Decision Making
ToC = Totality of Circumstances

Change in Behavior Doom Loop
(Chapter 3)

1. Suicidal Statement or Suicidal Behavior
2. Showing Signs of Research, Planning, Preparation
3. A Surge in Acquiring Weapons
4. Farewell Statements, Videos, Notes, Etc.

Ten Risk Factor Characteristics
(Chapter 3)

1. History of substance abuse
2. Specific and direct threats
3. Past conflicts of violence with coworkers
4. Preoccupation with violence
5. Prior convictions for violent crime
6. Difficulty with anger management
7. Increased belligerence or hypersensitivity to criticism
8. Extreme disorganization
9. Homicidal or suicidal comments or threats
10. Any other noticeable changes in behavior

14 Behaviors that Elicited Concern, U.S. Secret Service (Chapter 3)

1. Social media posts with alarming content
2. Escalating anger or aggressive behavior
3. Changes in behavior and appearance
4. Expressions of suicidal ideations
5. Writing about violence or weapons
6. Cutting off communications
7. Inappropriate behavior toward the opposite gender
8. Stalking and harassing behaviors
9. Increased depression
10. Increased drug use
11. Erratic behavior
12. Purchasing weapons
13. Threats of domestic violence
14. Acting paranoid

Five Imminent Threat Indicators
(Chapter 3)

1. Apparel

2. Actions

3. Demeanor

4. Eyes

5. Body Language

Seven Vulnerable Locations Facing a Threat of Active Shooters
(Chapter 4)

1. Commercial Areas

    a. Businesses Open to the Public

    b. Businesses Closed to the Public

    c. Malls

2. Educational Environments

    a. Pre-kindergarten through 12th grade

    b. Institutions of higher learning

3. Open Space Locations

4. Health Care Facilities

5. Government Facilities

    a. Military

      b.   Other government properties

6.   Places of Worship

7.   Residences

Four Categories of Hazards
(Chapter 4)

Category #1 Natural Hazard
• Earthquakes
• Tornadoes
• Lightning
• Severe Wind
• Hurricanes
• Floods
• Wildfires
• Extreme Temperatures
• Landslides or Mudslides
• Tsunamis
• Volcanic Eruptions
• Winter Precipitation

Category #2 Technological Hazards

- Explosions or accidental release of toxins from industrial plants
- Accidental release of hazardous materials from within a school such as gas leaks or laboratory spills
- Hazardous materials released on major highways or railroads
- Radiological releases from nuclear power stations
- Dam failure
- Power failure
- Water failure

Category #3 Biological Hazards

- Infectious diseases such as pandemic influenza, extensively drug-resistant tuberculosis, staphylococcus aureus, or meningitis
- Contaminated food outbreaks, including salmonella, botulism, and e. coli
- Toxic materials present in laboratories such as anthrax, botulism, brucellosis, plague, smallpox, tularemia, viral hemorrhagic fevers
- Chemical agents

Category #3 Biological Hazards

- Blisters
- Blood
- Choking/lung/pulmonary episodes
- Incapacitating gasses, such as nerve or tear gas
- Vomit

Category #4 Adversarial and Human Caused Hazards

- Fire
- Active shooters
- Criminal threats or actions
- Gang violence
- Bomb threats
- Domestic violence and abuse
- Cyber attacks
- Suicide
- Stationary vehicle bomb
- Attack with small arms
- Hydrogen sulfide ("stink bomb")
- Forced entry at night to damage property
- Electronic attack to destroy or alter records
- Unauthorized entry (forced or covert)

Three Incident Types
(Chapter 4)

1. Targeted Attacks
2. Group Attacks
3. Random Attacks

Four Broad Categories of Workplace Violence
(Chapter 5)

1. Absolute Strangers
2. Relatives, Personal Relationships
3. Employees and Supervisors
4. Customers, clients or patients

12 Workplace Violence Risk Factors
(Chapter 5)

1. People
2. Wait Time
3. Flow of Visitors
4. Location
5. Neighborhood
6. Perception

7. Workplace Design

8. Poor Internal Conditions

9. Working Conditions

10. Communication

11. Prevalence of Weapons

12. Proximity to Others

15 Possible Stressors in Perpetrators (Silver, A Study of the Pre-Attack Behaviors of Active Shooters in the United States Between 2000 – 2013, 2018)
(Chapter 6)

According to the FBI's research, "stressors" provide insight to possible motivations for a person to commit a crime. Stressors are invisible and hard to detect unless you are at least somewhat familiar with the person who may be exhibiting them. They are, "physical, psychological, or social forces that place real or perceived demands/pressures on an individual and which may cause psychological and/or physical distress. Stress is considered to be a well-established correlate of criminal behavior." (Felson, 2012)

#	Stressor	Definition
1	**Abuse of illicit drugs or alcohol**	Difficulties caused by the effects of drugs/alcohol and/or frustrations

#	Stressor	Definition
		related to obtaining these substances.
2	**Civil legal problems**	Being party to a non-trivial lawsuit or administrative action.
3	**Conflict with friends/peers:**	General tension in the relationship beyond what is typical for the active shooter's age or specific instances of serious and ongoing disagreement.
4	**Conflict with other family members:**	General tension in the relationship beyond what is typical for the active shooter's age, or specific instances of serious and ongoing disagreement.
5	**Conflict with parents:**	General tension in the relationship beyond what is typical for the active shooter's age, or specific instances of serious and ongoing disagreement.
6	**Criminal legal problems**	Arrests, convictions, probation, parole.
7	**Death of friend/relative**	Death that caused emotional or psychological distress.
8	**Financial strain**	Related to job loss, debt collection, potential or actual eviction, inability to pay normal and usual daily bills.
9	**Job-related problems**	Ongoing conflicts with co-workers or management, pervasive poor performance evaluations, or disputes overpay or leave.

#	Stressor	Definition
10	**Marital problems/conflict with intimate partner(s)/divorce or separation:**	Difficulties in the relationship that were a consistent source of psychological distress and/or which did or were likely to lead to the end of the relationship or the desire to end the relationship.
11	**Mental health problems:**	Symptoms of anxiety, depression, paranoia, or other mental health concerns that have a negative effect on daily functioning and/or relationships.
12	**Other:**	Any other circumstance causing physical, psychological, or emotional difficulties that interfere in a non-trivial way with normal functioning in daily life.
13	**Physical injury:**	Physical condition/injury that significantly interfered with or restricted normal and usual activities.
14	**School-related problems:** **or** **Conflict at school**	Conflicts with teachers and staff that go beyond single instances of minor discipline; pervasive frustration with academic work; inability to follow school rules. or

#	Stressor	Definition
		General tension in the schools beyond what is typical for the active shooter's age, or specific instances of serious and ongoing disagreement
15	**Sexual stress/frustration**	Pronounced and ongoing inability to establish a desire

*21 **Potential Concerning Behaviors*** (Silver, A Study of the Pre-Attack Behaviors of Active Shooters in the United States Between 2000 – 2013, 2018)

(Chapter 6)

Concerning behaviors are observable behaviors exhibited by the active shooter. The Concerning behaviors were identified by the FBI.

#	Concerning Behavior	Definition
1	**Amount or quality of sleep**	Unusual sleep patterns or noticeable changes in sleep patterns.
2	**Anger**	Inappropriate displays of aggressive attitude/temper.
3	**Change, escalation, or contextually**	Interest in or use of firearms that appears unusual given the

#	Concerning Behavior	Definition
	inappropriate firearms behavior	active shooter's background and experience with firearms.
4	**Changes in weight or eating habits**	Significant weight loss or gain related to eating habits.
5	**Hygiene or personal appearance**	Noticeable and/or surprising changes in appearance or hygiene practices.
6	**Impulsivity**	Actions that in context appear to have been taken without usual care or forethought.
7	**Interpersonal interactions**	More than the usual amount of discord in ongoing relationships with family, friends, or colleagues.
8	**Leakage**	Communication to a third-party of the intent to harm another person.
9	**Mental health**	Indications of depression, anxiety, paranoia or other mental health concerns.
10	**Other**	Any behavior not otherwise captured in above categories that causes more than a minimal amount of worry in the observer.
11	**Physical aggression**	Inappropriate use of force; use of force beyond what was usual in the circumstances.

#	Concerning Behavior	Definition
12	**Physical health**	Significant changes in physical well-being beyond minor injuries and ailments.
13	**Quality of thinking or communication**	Indications of confused or irrational thought processes.
14	**Risk-taking**	Actions that show more than a usual disregard for significant negative consequences.
15	**School performance**	Appreciable decrease in academic performance; unexplained or unusual absences.
16	**Sexual behavior**	Pronounced increases or decreases in sexual interest or practices.
17	**Threats/Confrontations**	Direct communications to a target of intent to harm. May be delivered in person or by other means (e.g., text, email, telephone).
18	**Use of illicit drugs or illicit use of prescription drugs**	Sudden and/ recent use or change in use of drugs; use beyond social norms that interferes with the activities of daily life.
19	**Use or abuse of alcohol**	Sudden and/or recent use or changes in use of alcohol; use beyond social norms that

#	Concerning Behavior	Definition
		interferes with the activities of daily life.
20	**Violent media usage**	More than a usual age-appropriate interest in visual or aural depictions of violence.
21	**Work performance**	Appreciable decrease in job performance; unexplained or unusual absences.

Eight Benefits of Safety and Security Professional Development
(Chapter 7)

1. Introduce the element of risk and emergency response procedures.

2. Show you truly care for their safety and increase staff productivity. They will learn how to react to unexpected environmental situational changes.

3. Comply with federal and state laws.

4. Mitigate against the potential of a lawsuit or compensation claims.

5. Hedge against indirect costs and boost your brand image.

6. Build team cohesiveness and learn from mistakes in a low stress environment.

7. Build muscle memory through repetition.

8. Build a mental model on how to respond and pivot dependent on the situation.

Four Steps in the Problem-Solving Process (Chapter 7)

1. Identify the problem

2. Decide on a course of action

3. Generate alternative solutions

4. Implement solution

Four options to consider When reacting to an active shooter (Chapter 8)

1. Evade

2. Obstruct

3. Defend

4. Teamwork

12 physiological responses a person may feel during heightened levels of stress
(Chapter 8)

1. Sweating
2. Dry mouth
3. Rapid heart rate/Palpitations
4. Nervousness
5. Uncontrollable shaking
6. Uncontrollable trembling
7. Instability to make decisions
8. Warm sensation over your body
9. Restricted breathing
10. Nausea/Upset stomach
11. Muscle tension
12. Loss of fine motor skills such as finger dexterity

Box Breathing: Four steps to optimal performance
(Chapter 8)

1. Breathe in for four seconds
2. Hold your breath for four seconds
3. Breathe out for four seconds
4. Hold your breath for four seconds

Appendix B: Notes and Links

1. List of 277 Active Shooter Incidents from 2000 to 2018 as of April 2019. (U.S. Department of Justice, 2019)

    This link contains a document with a list of 277 active shooter incidents in the United States that have been identified by the FBI from 2000 through the end of 2018.

    https://www.fbi.gov/file-repository/active-shooter-incidents-2000-2018.pdf/view

    For additional information related to each incident, please refer to the separate studies conducted by the FBI
    - *A Study of Active Shooter Incidents in the United States Between 2000 and 2013*
    - *Active Shooter Incidents in the United States in 2014 and 2015*
    - *Active Shooter Incidents in the United States in 2016 and 2017*
    - *Active Shooter Incidents in the United States in 2018.*

About the Author

 Luis A. Ramirez is the Founder and CEO of Fidelis NA, LLC and the Founder of Ramirez Consultancy, LLC (RCS). Fidelis provides customized risk mitigation and security management through the development of cost-efficient, non-invasive and personalized security solutions to improve the safety of personnel while mitigating the risks associated with the ownership of business current assets. RCS is a Veteran-Owned Small Business full-service strategic management consulting firm advising leaders on business operations that drive change and transformation with a focus on improving business functions.

Luis has over ten years of corporate business expertise in a wide variety of leadership positions, serving clients through business strategy and development, sales operations, remarketing operations, business analysis and risk management.

He began his corporate career in the luxury automotive industry as a Business Development Analyst working for Mercedes-Benz, USA, LLC (MBUSA). He then progressed to hold strategic positions as National Sales and Remarketing Analyst, Regional Business Analyst in General Management, Sales and Marketing

Program Management for Mercedes-Benz Financial Services, LLC (MBFS), to Asset Liquidation and Risk Management for both MBUSA and MBFS.

Luis is a strategic and diplomatic leader capable of managing and motivating cross-functional teams around a shared strategic vision. Luis' passion is cultivating relationships with customers, vendors, business leaders, and associates predicated on rapport and expertise.

Luis is a former United States Marine with extensive international business travel. He acquired his international experience while living and working abroad, which helped him develop a global perspective. He has experience working within security operations at U.S. Embassies across Europe and Asia.

Luis was the founder of Global CDH, a 501 (c)(3) non-profit organization helping children and families affected by diaphragmatic hernia.

He is an ultra-marathoner completing 50-mile and 100-mile races while learning from coming short in other races such as 200-milers. He is an avid traveler, who enjoys exploring cultures and loves helping others succeed.

Originally from Passaic, New Jersey, he has traveled to 28 countries and has previously lived in Moscow, Russia and Sarajevo, Bosnia-i-Herzegovina.

Education

OHIO STATE UNIVERSITY
Executive MBA

SETON HALL UNIVERSITY
MA, Economic Development Diplomacy and International Relationships

SETON HALL UNIVERSITY
BS, Diplomacy and International Relationships

PARK UNIVERSITY
AA, Criminal Justice Administration

Visit http://www.ramirezla.com/for additional information.

Bibliography

Global News . (2019, April 23). *Sri Lanka attacks: Police release footage, images of suspected suicide bombers.* Retrieved from YouTube.com: https://youtu.be/ED6-OPENVGg

U.S. Department of State. (2019, April 09). *Introduction of K Risk Indicator.* Retrieved from U.S. Department of State: https://travel.state.gov/content/travel/en/News/internati onal-travel-news/k-indicator.html

Abbinante, V. M. (2017). *Policy Decisions and Options-Based Responses to Active Shooters in Public Schools.* Retrieved from Semantic Scholar: https://pdfs.semanticscholar.org/59f0/cc3f144eb3b9ec306 a7bd8d51f93465d38e3.pdf

ABC 30. (2019, August 16). *Fresno Police arrest 15-year-old girl after she makes terror threats against her high school* . Retrieved from ABC, Inc., KFSN-TV Fresno: https://abc30.com/fresno-police-arrest-15-year-old-girl-after-she-makes-terror-threats-against-her-high-school/5470808/

abc15.com staff . (2019, August 16). *Valley teenager arrested after school threat posted online* . Retrieved from abc 15 Arizona: https://www.abc15.com/news/region-phoenix-metro/central-phoenix/valley-teenager-arrested-after-school-threat-posted-online

ALERRT. (2016). *Advanced Law Enforcement Rapid Response (ALERRT) Active Shooter Data.* Retrieved from Characteristics of the Active Shooter: http://www.activeshooterdata.org/the-shooter.html

Alsup, S. A. (2019, August 14). *Feds say in court docs that teen threatened agents and had stockpile of weapons and ammo* . Retrieved from

CNN:
https://apple.news/ADl6hbUU1R6y_kopNHA9zDw

Andersen, T. (2013, September 18). *Navy Yard shooter had odd episode in R.I.* Retrieved from Boston Globe:
https://www.bostonglobe.com/metro/2013/09/17/navy-yard-shooter-reported-hearing-voices-newport-victim-with-mass-ties-mourned/E1PkNY5nHe3euHp3sQRd8O/story.html

Associated Press. (2006, 08 31). *Cops: N.C. suspect e-mailed Columbine official.* Retrieved from NBC News:
http://www.nbcnews.com/id/14591327/ns/us_news-crime_and_courts/t/cops-nc-suspect-e-mailed-columbine-official/#.XX_q0i2ZMWo

Averill, J. D. (2005, September). *Federal Building and Fire Safety Investigation of the World Trade Center Disaster: Occupant Behavior, Egress, and Emergency Communications.* Retrieved from National Institute of Standards and Technology:
http://www.mingerfoundation.org/downloads/mobility/nist%20world%20trade%20center.pdf

azfamily.com News Staff. (2019, August 19). *Phoenix man accused of threatening to blow up Army recruiting center .* Retrieved from AZFamily | 3TV, CBS 5:
https://www.azfamily.com/news/phoenix-man-accused-of-threatening-to-blow-up-army-recruiting/article_2ca10a4a-c2a3-11e9-b0bc-570318df8601.html

BabyBus. (2018, June 11). *Baby Panda's Fire Evacuation | Super Firefighter Rescue Team | Kids Safety Tips | BabyBus.* Retrieved from YouTube:
https://www.youtube.com/watch?v=1Gwz1kEFLl4

Baron, C. (2019, August 19). *POLICE: Man posts death threats after police altercation with dogs* . Retrieved from Claremore Daily Progress: https://www.claremoreprogress.com/news/police-man-posts-death-threats-after-police-altercation-with-dogs/article_f8a9ab8c-c295-11e9-8cac-c7f34027987d.html

Bates, T. L. (2019, August 09). *El Paso Shooting Suspect Told Police He Was Targeting 'Mexicans.' Here's What to Know About the Case.* Retrieved from Time: https://time.com/5643110/el-paso-texas-mall-shooting/

Baucum, E. (2018, November 05). *Gunman's mother-in-law opens up about Sutherland Springs church massacre.* Retrieved from News 4 San Antonio: https://news4sanantonio.com/news/local/gunmans-mother-in-law-opens-up-about-sutherland-springs-church-massacre

Bill Chappel, R. G. (2019, August 09). *Rifle-Carrying Man Faces Terrorism Charge After Causing Panic At Walmart In Missouri Facebook Twitter Flipboard Email* . Retrieved from NPR: https://www.npr.org/2019/08/09/749763786/rifle-carrying-man-arrested-after-causing-panic-at-walmart-in-missouri

Bill Hutchinson, A. K. (2019, August 05). *Alleged shooter cased El Paso Walmart before rampage that killed 22: Law enforcement officials.* Retrieved from ABC News: https://abcnews.go.com/US/death-toll-rises-22-el-paso-shooting-victims/story?id=64780680

Blair, J. P. (2014). *A Study of Active Shooter Incidents, 2000 - 2013.* Washington, D.C.: Texas State University and Federal Bureau of Investigation, U.S. Department of Justice.

Boyette, M. H. (2019, August 10). *An armed man who caused panic at a Walmart in Missouri said it was a 'social experiment,' police say.* Retrieved from CNN: https://apple.news/A9DoJdjzgSbqq78r5ikepPg

Brick, M. N. (2009, November 06). *Neighbor Says Hasan Gave Belongings Away Before Attack.* Retrieved from The New York Times: https://www.nytimes.com/2009/11/07/us/07suspect.html?mtrref=www.google.com&gwh=EFFC1262DD2F26E70BE590A57E3D7D41&gwt=pay&assetType=REGIWALL

Buncombe, A. (2015, June 29). *Dylan Roof: Experts believe Charleston shooting suspect was author of racist manifesto and 'self-radicalised' online.* Retrieved from Independent: https://www.independent.co.uk/news/world/americas/dylan-roof-experts-believe-charleston-shooting-suspect-was-author-of-racist-manifesto-and-self-10353971.html

Burnett, C. B. (2019, August 11). *Teen in custody after threat toward Oak Grove High School*. Retrieved from WMBF News: https://www.wlbt.com/2019/08/12/teen-custody-after-threat-toward-oak-grove-high-school/

Carlisle, Z. (2019, August 16). *Arrests made for Tupelo school threats.* Retrieved from WTVA News: https://www.wtva.com/content/news/TPSD-Arrests-made-in-Tupelo-school-threats--547051411.html

CBS News. (2003, 07 18). *School Board Meeting Attacked.* Retrieved from CBS News: https://www.cbsnews.com/news/school-board-meeting-attacked/

CBS News. (2005, 11 09). *Charges In Tenn. School Shooting.* Retrieved from CBS News:

https://www.cbsnews.com/news/charges-in-tenn-school-shooting/

CBS News. (2006, 08 24). *2 Dead In Vermont School Shooting* . Retrieved from CBS News: https://www.cbsnews.com/news/2-dead-in-vermont-school-shooting/

CBS News. (2018, February 22). *New York teen who helped thwart apparent school shooting plot: "It's about lives," Text messages allegedly sent by Jack Sawyer to Angela McDevitt.* Retrieved from CBS News: https://www.cbsnews.com/news/new-york-teen-hailed-as-hero-for-reporting-friend-allegedly-planning-school-shooting/

CBS News. (2019, June 2019). *Park cameras likely won't help Salt Lake City police find missing Utah college student.* Retrieved from CBS News: https://www.cbsnews.com/news/mackenzie-lueck-missing-salt-lake-city-police-cant-use-hatch-park-cameras/

Children's Defense Fund. (2018, September). *School Shootings Spark Everyday Worries: Children and Parents Call for Safe Schools and Neighborhoods.* Retrieved from Children's Defense Fund: https://www.childrensdefense.org/wp-content/uploads/2018/09/YouGov-SafeSchools-Final-Sep-18-2018.pdf

Christopher Bollinger, R. F.-T. (2018). *Violence Goes to College: The Authoritative Guide to Prevention, Intervention, and Response 3rd Edition.* Springfield, Illinois: Charles C Thomas Publisher Limited.

CNN. (2003, 10 20). *Sniper Trial in Virginia Beach, Virginia Opens* . Retrieved from CNN: http://transcripts.cnn.com/TRANSCRIPTS/0310/20/lad.11.html

Dakin Andone, A. V. (2019, August 19). *Man accused of threatening an Ohio Jewish center declared himself a white nationalist in a documentary, police say* . Retrieved from CNN: https://apple.news/A4NPldRVHQ7WGzKP8lVzmiA

Danziger, P. N. (2019, August 17). *Forbes.* Retrieved from As Pressure Mounts For Walmart To Stop Selling Guns, There Is A Workable Business Solution : https://www.forbes.com/sites/pamdanziger/2019/08/17/ as-pressure-mounts-for-walmart-to-stop-selling-guns-there- is-a-workable-business-solution/#829bb8d7e092

Darran Simon, C. (2019, August 21). *Chicago man arrested after allegedly threatening to kill people at women's reproductive health clinic.* Retrieved from CNN: https://apple.news/Av51sQKI4Rl6eY2SoXVrB4w

Deerwester, J. (2019, August 09). *Flight attendant arrested after passenger alerts United: She 'appears to be quite drunk'.* Retrieved from USA Today: https://www.usatoday.com/story/travel/airline- news/2019/08/09/united-gets-complaint-after-fight- attendant-appears-drunk/1964652001/

Dickey, F. (2013, 05 10). *Column: Killer recounts Santana High shooting.* Retrieved from The San Diego Union - Tribune: https://www.sandiegouniontribune.com/news/columnists /sdut-charles-andy-williams-santana-high-school-shooting- 2013may10-htmlstory.html

Dominguez. (1994). Can situation awareness be defined? *Situation Awareness: Papers and Annotated Bibliography. Report AL/ CF- TR-1994-0085*, 20.

Eli Rosenberg, M. B. (2017, November 07). *Texas church gunman escaped mental health facility in 2012 after threatening military superiors*. Retrieved from The Washington Post: https://www.washingtonpost.com/news/post-nation/wp/2017/11/07/as-texas-town-mourns-details-emerge-on-gunmans-methodical-tactics-in-church-massacre/

Endsley, M. R. (1995). Toward a theory of situation awareness in dynamic-systems. *Human Factors*, 32-64.

Enger, J. (2015, 03 18). *The shooting at Red Lake: What happened.* Retrieved from MPR News: https://www.mprnews.org/story/2015/03/18/red-lake-shooting-explained

Eric R. Donley, J. W. (2019, June 22). *Hemorrhage Control.* Retrieved from National Center for Biotechnology Information: https://www.ncbi.nlm.nih.gov/books/NBK535393/

Erin Texeira, G. K. (2001, 03 23). *5 Hurt in Gunfire at High School Near San Diego; Student Is Held* . Retrieved from Los Angeles Times: https://www.latimes.com/archives/la-xpm-2001-mar-23-mn-41660-story.html

Faith Karimi, H. Y. (2019, August 16). *The man accused of shooting 6 Philadelphia police officers 'should not have been on the streets,' DA says.* Retrieved from CNN: https://apple.news/AWXBCezDMQy2V8_Ttk_P_ag

FBI, D. (2019, April 10). *Active Shooter Incidents in the United States in 2018.* Retrieved from Federal Bureau of Investigation: https://www.fbi.gov/file-repository/active-shooter-incidents-in-the-us-2018-041019.pdf/view

Felson, R. O. (2012). Having a bad month: General versus specific effects of stress on crime, 28. *Journal of Quantitative Criminology*, 347-363.

Fieldstadt, M. (2019, March 1). *Student killed in UNC Charlotte attack hailed as a hero for fighting suspected shooter* . Retrieved from NBC News: https://www.nbcnews.com/news/us-news/2-killed-4-wounded-university-north-carolina-charlotte-shooting-identified-n1000626

Foster-Frau, S. (2018, 02 06). *Exclusive: Guilt and grief overwhelm the mother-in-law of the Sutherland Springs gunman* . Retrieved from San Antonio Express News: https://www.expressnews.com/news/local/article/Exclusive-Guilt-and-grief-overwhelm-the-12556616.php

FOX 17 NEWS. (2019, August 19). *Family: Man charged for online threats a former Marine* . Retrieved from Fox 17 West Michigan: https://fox17online.com/2019/08/19/msp-man-arrested-for-threatening-videos-towards-ferris-state-hospitals/

Gajanan, M. (2018, March 01). *Kroger Will No Longer Sell Guns to People Under 21* . Retrieved from TIME: https://time.com/5180844/kroger-fred-meyer-guns/

Garcia, D. (2019, 08 11). *Threat to "shoot up" Walmart lands Harlingen man with terrorist charge.* Retrieved from KVEO News: https://www.kveo.com/news/threat-to-shoot-up-walmart-lands-harlingen-man-with-terrorist-charge/

GlobalNews. (2019, 04 23). *Sri Lanka attacks: Police release footage, images of suspected suicide bombers* . Retrieved from YouTube: https://www.youtube.com/watch?v=8-Slx7MWJVU

Gonzalez, R. (2018, 04 03). *Suspect In YouTube Shooting Angry That Her Videos Had Been 'De-Monetized'.* Retrieved from NPR: https://www.npr.org/sections/thetwo-way/2018/04/03/599261148/active-shooter-reported-at-youtube-hq-in-san-bruno-calif

Haddon, H. (2018, March 01). *Kroger to Stop Selling Guns to Buyers Under 21* . Retrieved from The Wall Street Journal: https://www.wsj.com/articles/kroger-to-stop-selling-guns-to-buyers-under-21-1519911901

Halaschak, Z. (2019, August 05). *Florida man threatens to 'shoot up' Walmart in Tampa after being 'intrigued' by El Paso and Dayton massacres* . Retrieved from Washington Examiner: https://www.washingtonexaminer.com/news/florida-man-threatens-to-shoot-up-walmart-in-tampa-after-being-intrigued-by-el-paso-and-dayton-massacres

Hamilton, C. (2019, August 25). *Police: Man threatened to 'shoot up' workplace.* Retrieved from Cecil Daily: https://www.cecildaily.com/police_and_fire_beat/police-man-threatened-mass-violence-at-elkton-area-workplace/article_dab756dd-cacf-50ef-8bac-5250b5e206bb.html

Harlingen Police Department. (2019, August 10). *Terroristic Threat Arrest.* Retrieved from Harlingen Police Department Press Release: http://www.myharlingen.us/upload/page/0579/2019-0058.pdf

Hersher, R. (2016, 11 28). *Charleston Church Shooting Suspect Will Represent Himself In Death Penalty Trial.* Retrieved from National Public Radio, INC (NPR): https://www.npr.org/sections/thetwo-way/2016/11/28/503580432/charleston-church-shooting-suspect-will-represent-himself-in-death-penalty-trial

Holcombe, M. (2019, August 18). *A man is arrested after expressing interest in committing a mass shooting, FBI says* . Retrieved from

CNN: https://apple.news/AFAd3RHV-QPu5F8zO0038oQw

Ian Simpson, P. S. (2013, 09 25). *FBI releases video of 'delusional' Navy Yard shooter.* Retrieved from Reuters: https://www.reuters.com/article/us-usa-military-navyyard/fbi-releases-video-of-delusional-navy-yard-shooter-idUSBRE98O0XU20130925

Inc., A. (2019, February 04). *Alphabet Announces Fourth Quarter and Fiscal Year 2018 Results.* Retrieved from abc.xyz: https://abc.xyz/investor/static/pdf/2018Q4_alphabet_earnings_release.pdf

Joint Committee to Create a National Policy to Enhance Survivability from Intentional Mass Casualty Shooting Events. (2013, September 01). *Active Shooter and Intentional Mass-Casualty Events: The Hartford Consensus II* . Retrieved from Bulletin of the American College of Surgeons: http://bulletin.facs.org/2013/09/hartford-consensus-ii/

Jones, C. (2018, November 29). *Dick's Sporting Goods ban on some guns dented sales. But weaker gun market also took toll* . Retrieved from USA Today: https://www.usatoday.com/story/money/2018/11/29/gun-ban-dents-sales-dicks-sporting-goods/2152134002/

Kamal, M. (2019, August 14). *POLICE: GIRL, 15, ARRESTED FOR THREATENING TO 'SHOOT UP' ALBERT LEA HIGH SCHOOL.* Retrieved from KIMT 3 News: https://www.kimt.com/content/news/Police-Girl-15-arrested-for-threatening-to-shoot-up-Albert-Lea-High-School-542101931.html

Karanth, S. (2019, August 12). *Florida Man Arrested For Threatening To Shoot Up Walmart After El Paso Massacre* . Retrieved from

HuffPost News: https://www.huffpost.com/entry/white-supremacist-florida-arrested-threat-shooting-walmart_n_5d50ce3fe4b0fc06ace9ac46

Karanth, S. (2019, August 11). *Florida Man Arrested For Threatening To Shoot Up Walmart After El Paso Massacre* . Retrieved from The HuffPost: https://www.huffpost.com/entry/white-supremacist-florida-arrested-threat-shooting-walmart_n_5d50ce3fe4b0fc06ace9ac46

Kat Kerlin, D. M. (2006, 03 16). *Shooting shock.* Retrieved from News Review: https://www.newsreview.com/reno/shooting-shock/content?oid=48175

KATC News. (2019, May 13). *No charges filed after man barricaded himself in home.* Retrieved from KATC News: https://katc.com/news/around-acadiana/iberia-parish/2019/05/13/suspect-barricaded-in-house-two-schools-on-lock-down/

Kelly, R. W. (2012). *Active Shooter Recommendations and Analysis for Risk Mitigation.* New York, New York: New York City Police Department.

KELOLAND News. (2019, August 20). *Rapid City man arrested for threats, damages and drugs* . Retrieved from Keloland Television: https://www.keloland.com/news/local-news/rapid-city-man-arrested-for-threats-damage-and-drugs/

Khushbu Shah, S. C. (2019, 04 23). *Sri Lanka Easter Sunday attacks: what we know.* Retrieved from Vox Media: https://www.vox.com/2019/4/21/18509739/sri-lanka-easter-sunday-attacks-terrorist

KITV Web Staff. (2019, August 19). *Maui Police arrest 18-year-old for terroristic threatening* . Retrieved from KITV 4 Island News: https://www.kitv.com/story/40936679/maui-police-arrest-18yearold-for-terroristic-threatening

KLFY. (2018, 12 13). *Ville Platte police investigate campus threat posted on Instagram* . Retrieved from KLFY: https://www.klfy.com/news/ville-platte-police-investigate-campus-threat-posted-on-instagram/

Lankford, A. (2013). Mass shooters in the USA, 1966–2010: Differences between attackers who live and die. *Justice Quarterly*, 1-20.

Martin, J. (2019, August 20). *Truck Driver Arrested for Threatening Mass Shooting at Memphis Church: FBI*. Retrieved from TIME: https://time.com/5656681/memphis-church-shooting-threat/

Moser, L. N. (2019, July 17). *North Salt Lake will replace 'dummy' cameras at park where Mackenzie Lueck disappeared*. Retrieved from kls.com: https://www.ksl.com/article/46596293/north-salt-lake-will-replace-dummy-cameras-at-park-where-mackenzie-lueck-disappeared

Mullerat, R. (2010). *International Corporate Social Responsibility*. The Netherlands: Kluwer Law International BV, The Netherlands.

Nassauer, S. (2018, December 04). *How Dick's Sporting Goods Decided to Change Its Gun Policy* . Retrieved from The Wall Street Journal: https://www.wsj.com/articles/how-dicks-sporting-goods-decided-to-change-its-gun-policy-1543955262

Natalie Neysa Alund, K. B. (2019, August 01). *Southaven Walmart shooting: Two dead, at least two injured in workplace attack.* Retrieved from Commercial Appeal: https://www.commercialappeal.com/story/news/2019/07/30/southaven-mississippi-walmart-shooting-police-respond-report-active-shooter/1864992001/

Nina Keck, L. E.-C. (2019, May 28). *This Teen Planned A School Shooting. But Did He Break The Law? LISTEN· 5:33 .* Retrieved from NPR: https://www.npr.org/2019/05/28/724347494/this-teen-planned-a-school-shooting-but-did-he-break-the-law

Nottingham, H. K. (2019, August 18). *A man was arrested in Florida for threatening to open fire on a large crowd of people.* Retrieved from CNN: https://apple.news/AZ5dClYOuSXW1HW4awQvRcw

NPR News. (2009, November 11). *Walter Reed Officials Raised Concerns About Hasan.* Retrieved from National Public Radio, Inc (NPR): https://www.npr.org/templates/story/story.php?storyId=120325699

O'connor, C. H. (2007, April 16). *Virginia Tech Shooting Leaves 33 Dead .* Retrieved from The New York Times: https://www.nytimes.com/2007/04/16/us/16cnd-shooting.html?mtrref=www.google.com&assetType=REGIWALL

O'Kane, C. (2019, August 5). *Army soldier saves multiple children during El Paso rampage: "I did that because that is what I was trained to do".* Retrieved from CBS News: https://www.cbsnews.com/news/off-duty-army-soldier-

saves-multiple-children-during-el-paso-rampage-i-did-that-
because-that-is-what-i-was-trained-to-do/

Paul, D. (2019, August 26). *Harvey Weinstein's third indictment could
open the door for actress Annabella Sciorra to take stand*. Retrieved
from The Washington Post:
https://www.washingtonpost.com/arts-
entertainment/2019/08/26/harvey-weinsteins-third-
indictment-could-open-door-another-accuser-take-stand/

Post, T. (2003, 09 25). *Two boys shot at central Minnesota high school, one
dies; suspect in custody* . Retrieved from Minnesota Public
Radio:
http://news.minnesota.publicradio.org/features/2003/09/
24_ap_schoolshooting/

Ramirez, L. A. (2019). *Proactive State of Mind Situational Awareness and
Preparedness*. Columbus, Ohio: Self-Published.

Robles, F. (2015, June 20). *Dylann Roof Photos and a Manifesto Are
Posted on Website*. Retrieved from The New York Times:
https://www.nytimes.com/2015/06/21/us/dylann-storm-
roof-photos-website-charleston-church-shooting.html

Rocque, M. (2012). Exploring school rampage shootings: Research,
theory, and policy. *The Social Science Journal*, 49(3), 304-313.

Santora, M. (2004, 02 10). *Student Opens Fire at a High School Near
Albany, Hitting a Teacher* . Retrieved from The New York
Times:
https://www.nytimes.com/2004/02/10/nyregion/student-
opens-fire-at-a-high-school-near-albany-hitting-a-
teacher.html

Sari Horwitz, C. H. (2015, June 20). *What we know so far about
Charleston church shooting suspect Dylann Roof*. Retrieved from
The Washington Post:

https://www.washingtonpost.com/news/post-nation/wp/2015/06/20/what-we-know-so-far-about-charleston-church-shooting-suspect-dylann-roof/?noredirect=on

Schenck v. United States, 249 (U.S. 47, 49-51 1917).

Schmidt, C. (2019, June 22). *UA launched hostile workplace, sexual harassment probes in football equipment manager program.* Retrieved from tucson.com: https://tucson.com/sports/arizonawildcats/ua-launched-hostile-workplace-sexual-harassment-probes-in-football-equipment/article_e6a18623-3abd-519f-9dfa-647f178bd8ce.html

Silver, J. S. (2018). *A Study of the Pre-Attack Behaviors of Active Shooters in the United States Between 2000 – 2013.* Washington, D.C.: Federal Bureau of Investigation, U.S. Department of Justice.

Silver, J. S. (2018). *A Study of the Pre-Attack Behaviors of Active Shooters in the United States Between 2000 – 2013.* Washington, D.C.: Federal Bureau of Investigation, U.S. Department of Justice.

Staff, M. C. (2019, August 10). *Chronic stress puts your health at risk: Chronic stress can wreak havoc on your mind and body. Take steps to control your stress.* Retrieved from Mayo Clinic Healthy Lifestyle Stress management: https://www.mayoclinic.org/healthy-lifestyle/stress-management/in-depth/stress/art-20046037

Stafford, R. (2006, 11 18). *School Shooting at Case Western Reserve University.* Retrieved from NBC News: http://www.nbcnews.com/id/15767366/ns/dateline_nbc-

crime_reports/t/school-shooting-case-western-reserve-
university/#.XX_dai2ZMWp

Sutton, S. (2019, August 20). *Florida high school student arrested after
posting shooting threat on video game chat* . Retrieved from
WPTV 5 News:
https://www.wptv.com/news/state/florida-high-school-
student-arrested-after-posting-shooting-threat-on-video-
game-chat

Ta, T. (2019, August 12). *Charles Town man arrested for alleged terror
threats.* Retrieved from Nexstar Broadcasting, Inc.:
https://www.localdvm.com/news/west-virginia/charles-
town-man-arrested-for-alleged-terror-threats/

The American College of Surgeons. (2017). *Stop the Bleed, Save a Life.*
Retrieved from BleedingControl.org:
https://www.bleedingcontrol.org/-
/media/bleedingcontrol/files/stop-the-bleed-booklet.ashx

The American College of Surgeons. (n.d.). *BleedingControl.org.*
Retrieved from BleedingControl.org:
https://www.bleedingcontrol.org/

The Associated Press. (2002, 01 16). *Law School Shooter Arraigned.*
Retrieved from CBS News:
https://www.cbsnews.com/news/law-school-shooter-
arraigned/

The Associated Press. (2003, 04 25). *Middle School Boy Shoots His
Principal, Then Kills Himself.* Retrieved from The New York
Times:
https://www.nytimes.com/2003/04/25/us/middle-
school-boy-shoots-his-principal-then-kills-himself.html

The Associated Press. (2009, November 07). *Clear warning signs,
Hasan's colleague say.* Retrieved from NBC News:

http://www.nbcnews.com/id/33753461/ns/us_news-
tragedy_at_fort_hood/t/clear-warning-signs-hasans-
colleagues-say/#.XXwkIlB7kWo

The Associated Press. (2019, August 09). *Armed man at Walmart says
he was testing right to bear arms.* Retrieved from The
Associated Press:
https://www.apnews.com/d7b0e50de7ba4e059c5e6e6098d
eeda7

The Guardian, O. L. (n.d.). *FBI investigates website and manifesto linked
to Charleston shooting suspect Dylann Roof*. Retrieved from The
Guardian: https://www.theguardian.com/us-
news/2015/jun/20/fbi-investigates-website-manifesto-
charleston-shooting-suspect-dylann-roof

The Kansas City Star Editorial Board. (2019, August 02). *'It struck
me as funny': Wyandotte County didn't take battery against employee
seriously BY THE KANSAS CITY STAR EDITORIAL
BOARD Read more here:
https://www.kansascity.com/opinion/editorials/article233443172.
html#storylink=cpy*. Retrieved from The Kansas City Star:
https://www.kansascity.com/opinion/editorials/article233
443172.html

The Monitor. (2019, August 8). *Weslaco police charges 13-year-old in
Walmart threat case* . Retrieved from The Monitor:
https://www.themonitor.com/2019/08/08/weslaco-
police-charges-13-year-old-walmart-threat-case/

TOMS. (n.d.). *End Gun Violence Together We're Taking A Stand On
Issues That Matter.* Retrieved from TOMS:
https://stories.toms.com/EGV-Giving/index.html

U.S. Attorney's Office District of Nevada. (2019, August 09). *Las
Vegas Man Charged With Possession of Illegal Firearms And*

Destructive Devices . Retrieved from United States Department of Justice: https://www.justice.gov/usao-nv/pr/las-vegas-man-charged-possession-illegal-firearms-and-destructive-devices

U.S. Department of Justice. (2018). *Active Shooter Incidents in the United States in 2016 and 2017*. Washington, D.C.: the Advanced Law Enforcement Rapid Response Training (ALERRT) Center at Texas State University and the Federal Bureau of Investigation.

U.S. Department of Justice. (2018). *Active Shooter Incidents in the United States in 2018*. Washington, D.C.: the Advanced Law Enforcement Rapid Response Training (ALERRT) Center at Texas State University and the Federal Bureau of Investigation.

U.S. Department of Justice. (2019). *2000 to 2018 Active Shooter Incidents*. Washington, D.C.: U.S. Department of Justice, Federal Bureau of Investigation.

U.S. Department of Justice. (2019). *Active Shooter Incidents in the United States in 2018*. Washington, D.C.: Advanced Law Enforcement Rapid Response Training (ALERRT) Center at Texas State University and the Federal Bureau of Investigation.

U.S. Secret Service. (2019, July). *United States Secret Service National Threat Assessment Center Mass Attacks in Public Spaces - 2018*. Retrieved from United States Secret Service National Threat Assessment Center: https://www.secretservice.gov/data/press/reports/USSS_FY2019_MAPS.pdf

United States Congress. (2019). *Public Law 112–265: Congress*. Retrieved from United States Congress:

https://www.congress.gov/112/plaws/publ265/PLAW-112publ265.pdf

US Attorney's Office Southern District of Florida. (2019, August 20). *Maryland Man Arrested for Making Multiple Threats to Injure and Kill Hispanics* . Retrieved from US Department of Justice: https://www.justice.gov/usao-sdfl/pr/maryland-man-arrested-making-multiple-threats-injure-and-kill-hispanics

USDOL BLS. (2018, November 8). *EMPLOYER-REPORTED WORKPLACE INJURIES AND ILLNESSES – 2017.* Retrieved from News Release BLS: https://www.bls.gov/news.release/pdf/osh.pdf

USDOL. (n.d.). *Workplace Violence.* Retrieved from Occupational Safety and Health Administration: https://www.osha.gov/SLTC/workplaceviolence/

Walker, I. (2019, June 30). *Your Business Can't Afford To Ignore The Risks Of Workplace Violence Any Longer.* Retrieved from Forbes: https://www.forbes.com/sites/ivywalker/2019/06/30/workplace-violence/#7c7929e817f2

Walmart Inc. (2019, August 19). *Second Quarter Fiscal Year 2020 Earnings August 15, 2019.* Retrieved from Walmart Inc.: https://corporate.walmart.com/media-library/document/q2-fy20-management-summary/_proxyDocument?id=0000016c-932e-dafb-a57f-f37efbfa0000

Weise, K. (2019, January 16). *Microsoft Pledges $500 Million for Affordable Housing in Seattle Area.* Retrieved from The New York Times: https://www.nytimes.com/2019/01/16/technology/micro

soft-affordable-housing-
seattle.html?elqTrackId=14566dd7c4dc493ca22443a67db2b
0de&elq=eefc450eeb0a452f8a729b841bfda050&elqaid=21
989&elqat=1&elqCampaignId=10758

WFTS Digital Staff . (2019, August 10). *'Don't go to Walmart next
week:' Winter Park man arrested for posting threats online* .
Retrieved from ABC Action News:
https://www.abcactionnews.com/news/state/dont-go-to-
walmart-next-week-winter-park-man-arrested-for-posting-
threats-online

Wigglesworth, A. (2019, August 21). *Disgruntled cook with high-powered
guns threatened mass shooting at Long Beach hotel, police say.*
Retrieved from LA Times:
https://www.latimes.com/california/story/2019-08-
21/police-arrest-hotel-cook-allegedly-threatening-to-shoot-
up-marriott-long-beach

Wildeman, M. K. (2019, August 12). *MUSC investigating sexual assault
of one of its nurses at the Institute of Psychiatry*. Retrieved from
The Post and Courier:
https://www.postandcourier.com/health/musc-
investigating-sexual-assault-of-one-of-its-nurses-
at/article_8c51a226-bd1a-11e9-aea9-eb361b5af517.html

World Health Organization. (2002). *Framework Guidelines for
Addressing Workplace Violence in the Health Sector*. Retrieved
from World Health Organization:
https://www.who.int/violence_injury_prevention/violence
/interpersonal/en/WVguidelinesEN.pdf?ua=1&ua=1

WPTV Webteam . (2019, August 12). *Mom upset with rezoning
threatens shooting at Florida elementary school* . Retrieved from
ABC Action News:

https://www.abcactionnews.com/news/state/mom-upset-with-rezoning-threatens-shooting-at-florida-elementary-school

Yan, M. (2019, May 15). *Colorado shooting suspects each face 48 counts, including the 16-year-old who's charged as an adult.* Retrieved from CNN: https://www.cnn.com/2019/05/15/us/colorado-suspects-court-hearing-kendrick-castillo-memorial/index.html

Yglesias, M. (2015, June 20). *Charleston shooting suspect Dylann Roof's apparent manifesto surfaces.* Retrieved from Vox: https://www.vox.com/2015/6/20/8818389/dylann-roof-manifesto

Zegart, A. (2015). Insider Threats and Organizational Root Causes: The 2009 Fort Hood Terrorist Attack. *The U.S. Army Quarterly Parameters Vol. 45 No. 2 Summer 2015*, 35-46.

Zennie, A. D. (2019, August 09). *Dayton Shooting Lasted Just 32 Seconds and Left 9 Dead. Here's the Latest on the Tragedy.* Retrieved from Time: https://time.com/5643405/what-to-know-shooting-dayton-ohio/

Index

www.ingramcontent.com/pod-product-compliance
Lightning Source LLC
Chambersburg PA
CBHW051435250726

48655CB00001B/78